Emotionality

This book focuses on the projections of romantic love and its progression in a selection of popular romance novels and identifies an innovation within the genre's formula and structure. Taking into account Giddens's notion of 'confluent' love, this book argues that two forms of love exist within these texts: romantic and confluent love. The analysis of these love variants suggests that a continuum emerges which signifies the complexity but also the formation and progressive nature of the protagonists' love relationships. This continuum is divided into three stages: the pre-personal, semi-personal, and personal. The first phase connotes the introduction of the protagonists and describes the sexual attraction they experience for each other. The second phase refers to the initiation of the sexual interaction between the heroine and hero without any emotional involvement. The third and final phase begins when emotions such as jealousy, shame/guilt, anger, and self-sacrifice are awakened and acknowledged.

Eirini Arvanitaki received her PhD from the University of Hull, UK. Since then, she has taught at the University of Hull, the University of Liverpool, UK, the Hellenic Mediterranean University, Greece, and the University of Cyprus. Currently, she is teaching at the Hellenic Open University (School of Social Sciences). She has served as an Evaluator Expert of the Marie Skłodowska-Curie Postdoctoral Fellowships and has participated in several EU-funded projects. Her research interests lie in the fields of gender, sociology, social policy, popular romance fiction, gender studies, feminism, cultural sociology, and English literature. She is the author of *Masculinities in Post-Millennial Popular Romance* (Routledge) and a co-editor of three books on pay gap between genders and working women and motherhood.

Routledge Focus on Literature

Orality, Form, and Lyric Unity
Poetics of Michael Donaghy and Don Paterson
Beverley Nadin

Milton and Music
Seth Herbst

Forensic Storytelling and the Literary Roots of Early Modern Feminism
ReSisters
Barbara Abrams

Supernatural Creatures in Arabic Literary Tradition
Ahmed Al-Rawi

Writing In-between
Collaborative meaning making in performative writing
Nandita Dinesh

Billy Lynn's Long Halftime Walk
Flags, Football, and the NFL's "Foxy" Patriotism Problem
Lisa Ferguson

Bosnian Authors in a European Window
A Comparative Study
Keith Doubt

Contemporary Irish Masculinities
Male Homosociality in Sally Rooney's Novels
Angelos Bollas

Creative Writing & the Experiences of Others
Strategies for Outsiders
Nandita Dinesh

Emotionality
Heterosexual Love and Emotional Development in Popular Romance
Eirini Arvanitaki

For more information about this series, please visit: www.routledge.com/Routledge-Focus-on-Literature/book-series/RFLT

Emotionality

Heterosexual Love and Emotional Development in Popular Romance

Eirini Arvanitaki

NEW YORK AND LONDON

First published 2024
by Routledge
605 Third Avenue, New York, NY 10158

and by Routledge
4 Park Square, Milton Park, Abingdon, Oxon, OX14 4RN

Routledge is an imprint of the Taylor & Francis Group, an informa business

Library of Congress Cataloging-in-Publication Data
Names: Arvanitaki, Eirini, author.
Title: Emotionality : heterosexual love and emotional development in popular romance / Eirini Arvanitaki.
Description: New York: Routledge, 2024. | Series: Routledge focus on literature | Includes bibliographical references and index.
Identifiers: LCCN 2024005493 (print) | LCCN 2024005494 (ebook) | ISBN 9781032558301 (hardback) | ISBN 9781032558318 (paperback) | ISBN 9781003432487 (ebook)
Subjects: LCSH: Romance fiction--History and criticism. | Fiction--Technique.
Classification: LCC PN3448.L67 A77 2024 (print) | LCC PN3448.L67 (ebook) | DDC 809.3/85--dc23/eng/20240206
LC record available at https://lccn.loc.gov/2024005493
LC ebook record available at https://lccn.loc.gov/2024005494

ISBN: 9781032558301 (hbk)
ISBN: 9781032558318 (pbk)
ISBN: 9781003432487 (ebk)

DOI: 10.4324/9781003432487

Typeset in Times New Roman
by Deanta Global Publishing Services, Chennai, India

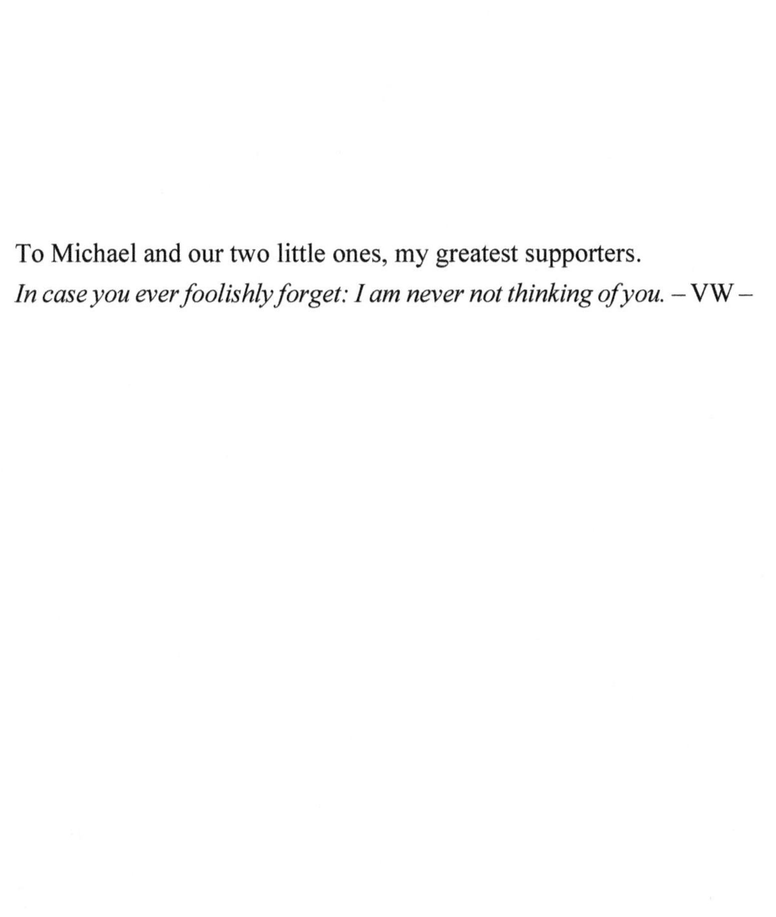

To Michael and our two little ones, my greatest supporters.

In case you ever foolishly forget: I am never not thinking of you. – VW –

Contents

Acknowledgements

This book was written in the very early hours. When the house was quiet and the outside world ceased to roar. Once it started, it became a task to be accomplished. Despite the exhaustion, the sleepless nights, and the obstacles, you helped me see it through, you never lost faith in me. For this, Michael, I am grateful. You are the driving force behind it. This book is dedicated to you and our little ones, G. and O., my raison d'être.

A great big and heartfelt thank you goes to my parents, O. and E., for being there in any way possible and supporting me all the way.

Last but not least, this book is also dedicated to the late Valia Sapountzaki (1966–2015) – a dear and trusting friend, a great teacher, a critical thinker, an extraordinary person.

To all of you, thank you.

Introduction

Romance is a genre which appears to have been treated less seriously than any other in literary studies (Regis 2003: xi–xiii). One of the reasons for this view is the genre's association with mass culture and production. Mass culture products aim at generating profit. In order to do so, they appeal to "the lowest common denominator" (Hollows 2000: 71). Unlike with highbrow literature, some critics view romance novels as products which could be easily and effortlessly consumed and please (passive) consumers without troubling their minds. Similarly, in mass culture debates there exists an equation of mass culture with feminine qualities and an inferior status[1] whereas highbrow literature and high art are associated with masculinity (Huyssen 1986: 196). With regard to romance, this view was adopted by many as it is a form of literature mainly written by women for women (Selinger and Frantz 2012: 3). Moreover, the contents of popular romances were considered to support and encourage a male-dominated culture (patriarchy).

What turned the attention of critics and feminists to romance fiction was not only the increased interest and mass production of the novels, but also the Women's Movement, and particularly second-wave feminism (which attempted to fight social and cultural gender inequality). These two events fuelled discussions on the notion of patriarchy which appears to be perpetuated through the pages of the romance narrative. Academics and feminists saw popular romance fiction as an attempt to entice women back into a patriarchal environment and a subordinate position in comparison to men. For example, Rosalind Coward writes that in romances the qualities of power and authority ascribed to the hero are adored and the representation of heroes bears resemblance to "a world before any struggles for autonomy has [*sic*] occurred" (1985: 191). At some point in the novels, the heroines may

DOI: 10.4324/9781003432487-1

strive for independence through employment, or against men (based on negative experiences of the past); however, the novels conclude with their [heroines'] surrender to the dominant hero. More specifically, she notes that

> what attracted them in the first place were precisely all the attributes of the unreconstructed patriarch. The qualities which make these men so desirable are, actually, the qualities which feminists have chosen to ridicule: power (the desire to dominate others); privilege (the exploitation of others); emotional distance (the inability to communicate); and singular love for the heroine (the inability to relate to anyone other than the sexual partner).
>
> (192)

Like Coward, Ann Rosalind Jones states that the underlying patriarchal message that romance narratives carry is that "the greatest goal and pleasure in women's life is the love of a good man" (1986: 211). Although she acknowledges that the romance novels of this period (the eighties) incorporate some feminist ideas (for example, women and work, their financial independence, and their more progressive attitudes in terms of approaching and pursuing the hero), she posits that these references (to feminism) seem to contradict the romance paradigm:

> the demand to be employed in a job worth a lifetime's concentration and to be loved, to be gratified as a working and desiring subject, sits uneasily with the prevailing convention through which the miraculous appearance of a man whose worldly millions and erotic genius solve all problems of identity and pleasure for the heroine once he admits that she is his one and only love.
>
> (204)

In fact, "Mills & Boon uses women's work merely *cosmetically*, to construct a glamorous opening identity for its heroines: they are actresses, singers, lawyers, public relations consultants, advertising designers" (206) (emphasis added). For the love conflict and story to unfold "the job that gives the heroine glamor must always be temporary" (207). With the dismissal of the heroine's job comes her subordination to a man and the reinforcement of patriarchy camouflaged as a reward (i.e. marriage to a wealthy man who takes care of her needs). In these romances "the good old days overpower any possibility of a new woman's era" (208). What Jones suggests here is that the romance novels embrace feminist elements with the purpose of enhancing the heroine's depiction. However, these elements are easily and quickly undermined in favour of the patriarchal messages they carry.

For these critics, romance is "a ghetto which imprisons women" (Hollows 2000: 68), hence the feminist slogan "it starts when you sink into his arms and ends with your arms in his sink" (Jackson 1993: 204). Because of the romantic elements embodied in them, novels were also considered a temptation that would distract women from their goals and ambitions. Some feminists (Firestone, Greer, Millett, among others) propose that if "housewives" refrain from their addiction to popular culture (in this case, reading romances) and turn their attention to feminist works, they may eradicate their "false consciousness". By doing so, they would join feminists in their effort to oppose patriarchy (Jackson 1995: 50).

In reference to the romance and women, some feminists (e.g. Modleski, Greer) describe romance fiction readers as victims of deception, and romance novels are "dope for dupes" (50). Equally, Tania Modleski equates the heavy (and, according to her, addictive) reading practices of such narratives to a "narcotic" ([1982] 1996: 57). Interestingly, Germaine Greer also uses the term 'housewives' when referring to readers of popular romance fiction. She excoriates the romance novel and labels it as "the escapist literature of love and marriage voraciously consumed by housewives" (1970: 214). On that note, the term 'housewife' describes an inactive, self-insufficient, naïve individual who is unable to distinguish between reality and fantasy. Additionally, Shulamith Firestone understands the romance as the result of power inequality between the two sexes ([1970] 2001: 130). Like Firestone, Modleski posits that the heroine in the end of popular narratives " is disfigured, dead, or at the very least, domesticated. And her downfall is seen as anything but tragic" ([1982] 1996: 12). Kate Millett suggests that "love is the only circumstance in which the female is (ideologically) pardoned for sexual activity" (1970: 37) and, with regard to the hero of the novels, Greer theorises that he is what "women have chosen for themselves. The traits invented for him have been invented by women cherishing the chains of their bondage" (1970: 202). Ann Barr Snitow takes a slightly different stance and appears shrewd when saying that novels "are neither an effective top down propaganda effort against women's liberation, nor a covert flowering of female sexuality" (1979: 143).

David Margolies (1982), on the one hand, disagrees with the way male domination and the female obsession with finding a man are presented as the norm in romance narratives. Moreover, he attacks romance novels by claiming that the attitude of the hero and heroine in the novels (i.e. male aggression and female obsession) is already accepted by the audience and therefore preserves and reinforces patriarchal views. On the other hand, he supports the idea that what romance reading offers to women is an opportunity to express feelings and emotions which are repressed in their daily routine (a conclusion also reached by Janice Radway). For Kay Mussell, romantic love functions as a refuge from the challenges that feminism might bring. Romance, she argues, is a safe and effortless choice that preserves the subordinate position of women in society. She supports her view with the following comment: "romances are adolescent dramas that mirror the infantilism of women in a patriarchal culture" (1984: 184).

The characterisation of romance fiction as an archetypal, monotonous, and fixed ideology, the unquestionable acceptance of this ideology by readers who seem unable to make a distinction between reality and fantasy, and the confusion of the context for the actual experience were only some of the issues raised in the negative critiques that the genre received. The conclusion that the above critics seem to draw is that in a patriarchal environment, romance operates as a legitimate medium through which the sexual and emotional exploitation of women is achieved (Hollows 2000: 72). In this regard, women reading these narratives appear to willingly submit to male domination and maintain the imbalance of power. It is because of this perception that critics did not focus on the benefits of reading romances for women. For them, romances are sources of evidence of female masochism as they portray women willingly accepting and adapting to a patriarchal way of life.

Although there is some scholarly interest in romance fiction that predates this time period,[2] it was in the 1980s that the bulk of academic works and in-depth investigations of the romance genre (and on its functions, association, and effects on women) emerged. *Loving with a Vengeance*, a work by Tania Modleski (1982), was one of the first texts which approached romance and its readership in a serious and academic manner. Her work discusses three forms of writing: soap operas, Harlequin romances, and Gothic novels. She argues that it is essential to comprehend the texts in order to perceive the possible solutions they offer to social concerns, and she opposes the idea that keeping women restricted in a domestic environment is the objective of the texts. Combining textual analysis with psychology and psychoanalysis, she aims to demonstrate how women attempt to apply the "utopian ideals" found in the novels to their everyday lives. She propounds that "the transformation of brutal (or, indeed, murderous) men into tender lovers, [and] the insistent denial of the reality of male hostility towards women" requires "an intensely active psychological process" and it is "as much a protest against as an endorsement of the feminine condition" (58), a point also made by Janice Radway. What derives from her analysis is that romance readers are not passive consumers. On the contrary, they actively engage with the text by trying to adapt its elements to their lives to improve their living circumstances. Moreover, Radway suggests that the act of reading (of these narratives) can be seen as a rejection but also acceptance of patriarchy by women.

Reading the Romance: Women, Patriarchy, and Popular Culture (Janice Radway 1984) is a seminal study which holds a very prominent position in the academic literature. Critics in their reviews praise her thought-provoking and innovative contribution to the field. Cathy Davidson, for instance, states that "Radway's study convincingly assesses the mechanisms by which a culture makes its culture" (Davidson 1985: 527). Cawelti pays his tribute to Radway's study by arguing that the "book [is] by far the best explanation of the cultural significance of the romance genre yet published" (Cawelti 1986: 1513).

Radway engaged a group of 42 middle-class female romance readers to conduct her research. The purpose of her research was to identify "how actual readers interpret the actions of principal characters, how they comprehend the final significance of the narrative resolution and, perhaps most important, how the act of repetitively encountering this fantasy fits within the daily routine of their private lives" (Radway 1983: 56). A variety of methods – ethnographic interviews, open-ended discussions as well as questionnaires, content analysis, and the theory of reader–response criticism – were employed. Based on the preferences, reading practices, and interpretations of the participants, Radway "distinguish[es] analytically between the significance of the event of reading and the meaning of the text". Furthermore, she places great emphasis on the former (reading practices) given that it acts as a dynamic which intervenes in the social lives of women (Radway [1984] 1991: 7). Through her study she reaches the conclusion that romance novels are seen by some readers as a form of escape from the tensions and pressures of everyday life and by others as a means to satisfy their longing for caring and affection, a need for nurturing that they do not experience in their daily lives. Radway's research results could also be seen as paradoxical. The romance narrative acts "as conservator of the social [patriarchal] structure and its legitimizing ideology" ([1984] 1991: 73) is expressed through elements such as the heterosexual monogamous relationship and the betrothal/marriage and simultaneously it [the romance novel] and is seen as a means of expressing women's desires and concerns. In other words, the readers' identification with the heroine and her pursuit of love (which concludes with a happily-ever-after ending) confirms both their and the genre's resistance to and acceptance of patriarchy. Radway argues that although the narratives display a patriarchal matrix by placing women in a subordinate position in relation to men, they also disclose ways to resist it. She states:

> [T]he romance, which is never simply a love story, is also an exploration of the meaning of patriarchy for women. As a result, it is concerned with the fact that men possess and regularly exercise power over them in all sorts of circumstances. By picturing the heroine in relative positions of weakness, romances are not necessarily endorsing her situation, but examining an all-too-common state of affairs in order to display possible strategies for coping with it.
>
> (Radway [1984] 1991: 75)

Overall, her research serves as an important breakthrough in the romance genre and challenges critics, scholars, and feminists to reevaluate and reconsider their view of romance novels as "backlash against feminism" and underlines the need for a better comprehension of romantic fiction and the actual reader who is formed through the narratives (Radway [1984] 1991: 19).

The idea of the need for nurturance derives from Nancy Chodorow's work *The Reproduction of Mothering: Psychoanalysis and the Sociology of Gender* (1978) which Radway uses as her theoretical framework. According to Chodorow's analysis of social and familial formation in the twentieth century, the reproduction of individuals falls entirely to women due to child care duties; "physically in their housework and child care, psychologically in their emotional support of husbands and their maternal relation to sons and daughters" (Chodorow 1978: 36). As a consequence of the way societal norms are structured, women experience an inequality in the act of reproduction. They are expected to reproduce others without being reproduced themselves. What romance novels offer to women is the fulfilment of a void caused by the asymmetry and/or absence of nurturance. From Radway's perspective, the female reader of the romance novel satisfies her needs by leaving her worries and duties aside and accepting a passive role which is offered in the romance. In this type of narrative, passivity refers to the moment when the hero realises his feelings about the heroine and she is given the chance to simply be the centre of his attention and receive his limitless affection and nurturance. Since the female reader identifies with the heroine of the novel, she also feels nurtured and reproduced.

Aside from the act of reading, women when pursuing emotional nurturance and support, resort to small communities or, in Radway's terms, "neighbourhood societies" that allow them to temporarily stand off from the familial environment, forget their reproductive duty and feel nurtured and supported by others (Radway [1984] 1991: 96). In the case of Radway's research subjects, a group of readers in Smithton could constitute such a community. Therefore, the significance of romance reading and small communities lies in what women receive: a temporary emotional comfort and fulfilment. Jean Radford echoes this point. Instead of seeing romantic fiction "as a packaged commodity relaying false consciousness to an essentially passive and foolish reader" she argues that although romance novels may include elements that support patriarchy, they concurrently create an imaginary environment that can meet most feminine daily needs (for example, nurturance) as well as divert and amuse (Radford 1986: 14).

Similar to Radway, Dixon's work *The Romance Fiction of Mills & Boon 1909–1990s* (1999) portrays romance novels as indicators of problems and difficulties that women have to deal with when living in a male-dominated world. Dixon arrives at the conclusion that at the end of the narratives – since the heroine triumphs as she changes the aggressive hero into a lovable partner – a state of equilibrium between the feminine and the masculine is established. Based on this equality she compares romance and feminist ideology and makes a bold and rather audacious assumption:

> [t]hey both have a Utopian vision of a society which puts women's desires first, where men adapt themselves to women's needs, and not vice versa, and where there is no perceived difference between

> the status and social position of men and women. Mills & Boon romances and feminism have differing political frameworks, but it may be that under the skin they are sisters. Feminism has many faces. Perhaps romance is one of them.
>
> (Dixon 1999: 195)

In a similar manner to Radway and Dixon's view of romances (i.e. as stories which touch on women's difficulties and issues regarding their daily lives and also as sources that may offer possible solutions), Alison Light perceives the act of romance reading to be:

> as much a measure of their deep dissatisfaction with heterosexual options as of any desire to be fully identified with the submissive versions of femininity the texts endorse. Romance imagines peace, security and ease precisely because there is dissension, insecurity and difficulty. In the context of women's lives, romance reading might appear [...] a sign of discontent and a technique for survival.
>
> (Light 1984: 22)

Additionally, romance for readers is a source of addressing the quest for sexual pleasure, especially when they are involved in an unsatisfactory marriage (22). In other words, novels usually recount a fairy tale, the progress of a relationship, deep and sincere feelings between two individuals, and tend to end just after betrothal (when real life and problems start). Romance readers are left "in a permanent state of foreplay [...] that for many women this is the best heterosexual sex they ever get" (23). If this is the case, and romance is a way of satisfying women's needs and expressing concerns and anxieties, then the repetition of romance formula and plot is what women tend to value.

Modleski views romance novels as a form of women's protest that hide elements of "a deep-seated desire for vengeance" (Modleski [1982] 1996: 45). By vengeance, the author refers to a profound wish of the heroine, and therefore women, for an opportunity to get the upper hand (over a male individual or a situation) in a patriarchal society. The notion of vengeance in novels is expressed through the heroine's desire to rebel against the hero and oppose his authority. To achieve this, the heroine often disappears, tries to commit suicide, or harms herself. This is the point where the hero realises how much she means to him. The goal of the heroine is now achieved through the pain and anxiety she puts the hero through. She has finally taken her revenge and made him feel emotions similar to hers. In romance novels, the 'deep-seated desire for revenge' for the heroine (and therefore the women readers) is quite bizarre as it does not derive from the hero's feelings of loss. Rather, this desire is satisfied through the taming of a hero. Like Radway, Dixon, and Light, Modleski identifies romances as both reinforcing and oppositional with regard to patriarchy. They [romances] support it by depicting heroines in subordinate positions but also resist it by illustrating heroines acting against the heroes' dominant behaviour.

The turn of the millennium has witnessed more academic engagement and insightful criticism in the discourse of romance. For example, a plethora of studies have emerged which focus on single romance authors (rather than assuming that all romance novels are the same), the differences between the various subgenres, and provide further engagement with feminist criticism and the romance genre.

As noted above, Regis perceives popular as well as canonical texts as literature and identifies the former as complex narratives. Opposing earlier views of romances as "easy to read pablum" (Snitow 1979: 309), "rigid" (Modleski 1982: 32), and with a "superficial plot development" (Radway [1984] 1991: 133), Regis suggests that the novels are "complex, formally accomplished, [and] vital" with a "form [that] is neither moribund nor corrupt" (2003: 45). Earlier critics propose that the dismissal of romances is based on "patriarchy's denial of women's right to explicate their own lives" (Mussell 1984:185). Regis repudiates this viewpoint. Instead, she advocates that they are "joyful in [their] celebration of freedom" (2003: 207). Distanced from the bourgeois values of the past, the featured heroines now enjoy their freedom as they can "make their own decisions, make their own livings, and choose their own husbands" (207). Frantz and Selinger's view of romance novels also differs from critics and scholars of the pre-millennium era. For them, romance narratives are "subtexts of power" (Frantz and Selinger 2012: 4) and as such they urge the academic community to study them "in search of subtexts, self-contradictions, and other complexities" (4). Moreover, they object to the stereotypical view of romance as 'light' reading infused with clichés and suggest instead that scholars, academics, bloggers, and fans now participate in an active and "conscious engagement with political issues and changes in the publishing industry" (9). What they claim is that romance readers are far from passive. They do not perceive these stories as texts read in order to simply derive pleasure or kill time.

Rather, they are active, well-informed – "they know the history and variety of the genre better, even now, than most academics who study it" (9–10) – and even act as reviewers of romances (10).

Frantz and Selinger's observation on the extensive knowledge of the romance readers on the genre is evident in the humorous work of Sarah Wendell and Candy Tan entitled *Beyond Heaving Bosoms: The Smart Bitches' Guide to Romance Novels*. Both Wendell and Tan, ardent supporters and readers of the popular romance fiction, reject the accusation that romance novels are all the same. According to Wendell and Tan, this unsupported assumption – that romances are characterised by a sameness and seen as "boring, trite, repetitive and banal" texts (2009: 124) – derives from the concept that all romances follow a specific formula. However, the existence of a formula does not signify a standardised production of romances as identical items. Rather, a formula for them refers to "a structure [and] a foundation of common elements to each novel" (i.e. happily-ever-after ending, love relationship). What makes each novel different and therefore non-formulaic is the manner in which "those elements are woven together into a delicious narrative". Romance, as they define it, is "the variations in the space between the narrative elements" (122).

What can be derived from the above is that romance appears to have made great strides: from being ridiculed, demonised, and seen as a means toward the subordination of women to being celebrated, openly enjoyed, scrutinised, and worthy of academic and scholarly attention.

With this in mind, the following analysis of the novels examined here marks an attempt to critically engage with the existing scholarship and to situate this book within the twenty-first-century popular romance literature. More specifically, *Emotionality: Heterosexual Love and Emotional Development* focuses on the relationship and specifically the emotional development of the protagonists and attempts to re-examine the projections of love shared by the protagonists of selected 'Modern' popular romance narratives. In line with Chris Weedon's belief that "[f]rom the classics of the cinema, which fill our television screens several times a week, to the massive industries in magazine and novel romances, we are offered remarkably timeless representations of femininity, masculinity and love" ([1987] 1997: 100), this book moves beyond the stereotype of the ideal and romantic relationship that exists between the heroines and heroes. That is not to say that it rejects the traditional idea of a romantic union and the emotional development of the protagonists. Instead, it identifies another projection of love (confluent) and investigates all the steps towards the happily-ever-after ending. While Pamela Regis has identified eight elements that together encompass this journey to marriage or betrothal (2003: 30–39), this book follows an alternative approach and – by taking into consideration Antony Giddens's work in *The Transformation of Intimacy* (1992) and his concept of 'confluent' love – it contributes to the existing romance literature by forming a novel continuum of the love relationship and distinguishes three main parts: the pre-personal, semi-personal, and personal. This three-stage development, in addition to the emotions triggered in all phases of a romance novel – from romantic jealousy, guilt, and anger to masochism and finally the realisation of love – is analysed in detail.

Love, and specifically romantic love, constitutes a central element in the romantic narratives. A growing number of post-millennial studies have examined the notion of romantic love in the romance context. Within these studies, love has been approached from different perspectives and in a variety of contexts: imperial,[3] postcolonial,[4] and religious,[5] to name but a few. Moreover, the concept of love has been discussed as a revolutionary and liberating force from patriarchal norms[6] and as an emotion shared between two individuals of the same sex.[7] As this book focuses on the investigation and analysis of the projections of love in romance narratives, the aim here is to critically engage with studies that examine the concept of romantic love *per se*.

In a published edited collection of essays entitled *Romance Fiction and American Culture: Love as the Practice of Freedom?* (Gleason and Selinger 2016), Catherine Roach examines romantic love and suggests that in popular culture love can be perceived as a form of bondage since it thrives on the constraint of freedom; when an individual is experiencing love, he/she sets aside everyone else, focuses on only one person ('the One'), and enters in a monogamous pair-bonding for the establishment of a possible happily-ever-after. Roach identifies two types of love as bondage: a good and a bad one. "Love as bad bondage" (2016: 376) does not free individuals, but rather subjects them to domination and oppression. This form of love "entail[s] bondage to an unworthy partner, bondage within cycles of abuse, bondage to low self-esteem such that one feels unworthy or unlikely to experience anything better in one's love life" (376). On the other hand, love as "good bondage" (as it is portrayed in popular romance novels) is simultaneously liberating and binding since, as Roach suggests

> love makes possible a very special and precious type of freedom – the freedom to give one's heart to a worthy other, to fulfil one's being in fully partnered union, to achieve one's highest and most complete self through the practice of true love.
>
> (377)

Roach's description of the type of love found in the romance narratives (i.e. as the practice of freedom) could be useful for an investigation of love and its effects on the individuals experiencing it. However, this analysis on romantic love is geared toward the different emotions the protagonists experience in the process of forming a romantic relationship.

In *The Transformation of Intimacy* (1992), Antony Giddens discusses two forms of love, the romantic and confluent love. For Giddens, romantic love goes hand-in-hand with intimacy, commitment, and monogamy, and is formed based on the emotional involvement of two individuals. Confluent love nourishes lust and sexual pleasure, focuses on the self,[8] and, in stark contrast to romantic love which carries the ideas of "for-ever" and "one-and-only" (61), it is firmly grounded on the concept of "until further notice" (63). According to Giddens, what distinguishes these two forms of love is that

> [r]omantic love is sexual love, but it brackets off the *ars erotica* [...] [whereas] confluent love for the first time introduces the *ars erotica* into the core of the conjugal relationship and makes the achievement of reciprocal sexual pleasure a key element in whether the relationship is sustained or dissolved.
>
> (62)

Based on the different nature of these love forms, Giddens posits that popular romance novels portray and reinforce a depiction of romantic love. Specifically, the heroine – through her ability to emotionally tame the hero – is the trigger for the emergence of mutual affection, the creation of a possible shared future (46). This book corroborates Giddens's view on romantic love and notes the agreement between an awakening of emotions, the realisation of love, and the formation of a romantic relationship (happily-ever-after ending). However, this analysis of popular romance novels challenges Giddens's argument (i.e. that romantic and confluent love are distinct forms [of love]) and instead shows that in a popular romance context not only can confluent and romantic love co-exist, but also that the former facilitates the development of the latter.

Lynne Pearce's work entitled *Romance Writing* (2007) examines the progress of romantic love, and especially the happily-ever-after ending of the romance stories. In Harlequin and Mills & Boon novels, the betrothal in the end receives the form of "an equal partnership" (Dixon 1999: 64) and Pearce illustrates it through the use of a mathematical equation ($x+y \rightarrow x'+y'$) which she uses as the baseline for her argument. Pearce argues that novels end with the "personal triumph" of the heroine over the hero (2007: 140). She reaches this conclusion by borrowing from Dixon who suggests that the aim of the heroine is not to find love, but "to *use* it" in order to "capture [...] the hero" in the process of her self-actualisation (141). Consequently, Pearce's algebraic formula alters to "$x+y > x' (-y)$ where 'x' is the superficially self-fulfilled heroine and 'y' the ultimately dispensable hero" (2007: 141). Therefore, and since the heroine puts herself first, their union is *not* an ideal romantic love since it lacks reciprocity (8). Pearce sees this type of romantic love as a means to an end for the heroine and defines it as follows: "Love which ends with the self, and not with the other, is also inevitably, the end of the story, the end of the relationship: a little – and maybe not so little – death" (141). Pearce also identifies "a new sexualized form of romantic love appeared to offer a way out; but it was [...] more often the way to the self and not to the other; the way to (orgasmic) oblivion, rather than meaningful relationality" (136).

Romantic love is also the main element under investigation in Susan Weisser's book *The Glass Slipper* (2013). Unlike Pearce who scrutinises the literary representation of love,[9] Weisser provides an analysis of the portrayal of love in popular culture and media.[10] Specifically, she draws attention to love in the twenty-first century which she defines as "a curious, distinctive mix of subversive and conservative, complex and tangled" (2013: 207). Weisser's argument is grounded in her "stages theory" of today's true (or ideal) love. She lists two stages; the first is characterised by passion, attraction, and an uncontrollable eruption of sexual desire whereas the second stage refers to a more mature form of romantic love: that one of companionship, friendship, caring, compatibility, affection, and loyalty (9). Weisser also notes that the second stage *could* (and in popular culture it is expected to) be the outcome of the first. Both scholars highlight the existence of a sexual attraction and passion with regard to romantic love. However, their views are contradictory: Pearce gives it a negative connotation – the concurrence of the realisation of love and the sexual consummation as well as the frequent and numerous sexual encounters between the protagonists of the romance novels portray romantic love as a "drug, and those addicted are ever in need of their next sexual fix" (2007: 139) – whereas Weisser perceives passion and desire as the initial steps towards a possible actualisation of a true and ideal form of romantic love. Unlike Weisser who identifies the sexual attraction and bodily desire as elements that may facilitate the formation of a romantic relationship, Giddens suggests that confluent love, although it holds a crucial role in a relationship, does not promise a shared future, duration of a relationship, or emergence of romantic love.

Emotionality: Heterosexual Love and Emotional Development investigates love and, more specifically, the emotional evolution of the protagonists towards their romantic union and the actualisation of romantic love. In line with Pearce's argument, this book acknowledges the *transient* existence of a 'new sexualised form of love' which it labels as confluent love. This type of a love relationship is purely based on the gratification of bodily desire (rather than emotional) of the protagonists. However, as *both* the hero and heroine (sexually) benefit from it and fulfil their carnal needs, the analysis offered here contrasts Pearce's (and subsequently Dixon's) views and suggests that the heroine is not using love to 'trap' the hero. Rather, it shows that the heroine falls victim of her emotions; although she becomes aware of an emotional awakening, she chooses to remain silent and suppress it in order not to lose the hero. It is only through (mostly the heroine's but also the hero's) self-sacrifice and a delay of one's own gratification that an (altruistic) romantic love relationship emerges between the protagonists. Moreover, although Weisser's work is a discussion of romantic love in a different context, the stages described in her 'stages theory' could be applied to romance fiction, and seem to bear a similarity to the last two parts of the love continuum constructed in the following pages (i.e. semi-personal and personal) in which carnal desire and passion (semi-personal relationship) gradually give way to an awakening of feelings and the realisation and actualisation of romantic love (personal relationship). Through an exploration of the emotional evolution of the protagonists, this book endeavours to extend Weisser's theory by identifying another part in the process of the construction of the romantic relationship; that of the pre-personal (i.e. the initial attraction that the protagonists experience based on each other's physical appearance and characteristics). Chapter 1 discusses the concept of 'love', and by drawing from various scholars in the fields of popular culture, popular fiction, and gender studies, a definition is formed. Moreover, a distinction is made between the two love variants (romantic and confluent) experienced by the fictional characters of the romance novels. Chapter 2 focuses on the love continuum formed; a continuum that illustrates the progress of the love relationship between the hero and heroine of these romance narratives. Furthermore, an attempt is made to map this continuum onto selected romance novels, and by doing so its different stages – pre-personal, semi-personal, and personal – are analysed in detail. At the third and final stage of this continuum, the awakened emotions (romantic jealousy, guilt and shame, anger, and altruistic love) that lead to the realisation of love are examined separately.

Notes

1 For instance, the linking of mass culture with feminine qualities is evident in Horkheimer and Adorno's work *Dialectic of Enlightenment*, who posit that mass culture "cannot renounce the threat of castration" ([1944] 1972: 141). In addition, in *The Uses of Literacy*, Richard Hoggart (1958) also discusses the transformation of the 'authentic' working class culture by mass culture into a passive 'inauthentic' mass and asserts that mass culture has the ability to emasculate.

2 For example, some of the work on romance fiction predating the 1980s is Rachel Anderson's *The purple heart throbs: the sub-literature of love* (1974) and Ann Barr Snitow's 'Mass market romance: pornography for women is different' (1979).

3 See Teo, H. (2014) "We have to learn to love imperially": love in late colonial and federation Australian romance novels. *Journal of Popular Romance Studies*, 4 (2). Available Online: http://jprstudies.org/2014/10/we-have-to-learn-to-love-imperially-love-in-late-colonial-and-federation-australian-romance-novelsby-hsu-ming-teo/ [Accessed 11/4/2014].

4 See, Philips, D. (2011) The empire of romance: love in a postcolonial climate. In Gilmour, R. & Schwarz, B. (eds.) *End of empire and the English novel since 1945*. Manchester: Manchester University Press, 114–133.

5 See Darbyshire, P. (2002) The politics of love: Harlequin romances and the Christian right. *The Journal of Popular Culture*, 35 (4), 75–87. Also, Rani, M. (2014) The conflict of love and Islam: the main ingredients in the popular Islamic novels of Malaysia. *South East Asia Research*, 22 (3), 417–433 and Rix, R. (2009) Love in the clouds: Barbara Cartland's religious romances. *Journal of Religion and Popular Culture*, 21 (2). Available Online: http://www.utpjournals.press/doi/abs/10.3138/jrpc.21.2.002 [Accessed 11/4/2016].

6 See Hardens, R. (2012) Borderlands of desire: captivity, romance and the revolutionary power of love. In Frantz, S. & Selinger, E. (eds.) *New approaches to popular romance fiction*. Jefferson, North Carolina and London: McFarland, 133–152.
7 See Ross, M. (2013) "What's love but a second hand emotion?" Man-on-man passion in the contemporary black gay romance novel. *Callaloo*, 36 (3), 669–678.
8 Bawin – Legros notes that this type of love brings forward a "new sentimental order" which derives from an "individualistic withdrawal into self" (2004: 242).
9 Starting from as early as the seventeenth century to the present day, Pearce identifies the different forms that romantic love has occupied in literary works (i.e. romantic love as a gift of companionship, immortality, self-sacrifice, and selfhood).
10 In her work, Weisser explores a variety of narratives as romantic stories (ranging from popular romance novels to Victorian women's magazines and from reality TV and Internet advertisements) and examines the idea of love from a sociological perspective (marriage, sexuality, gender).

Bibliography

Anderson, R. (1974) *The purple heart throbs: the sub-literature of love*. London: Hodder & Stoughton.

Bawin-Legros, B. (2004) Intimacy and the new sentimental order. *Current Sociology*, 52 (2), 241–250.

Cawelti, J. (1986) Reading the romance: women, patriarchy, and popular literature by Radway Janice. Reviewed in *Journal of Sociology*, 91 (6), 1512–1513.

Chodorow, N. (1978) *The reproduction of mothering: psychoanalysis and the sociology of gender*. Berkeley and Los Angeles: University of California Press.

Coward, R. (1985) *Female desires: how they are sought, bought and packaged*. New York: Weidenfeld.

Darbyshire, P. (2002) The politics of love: Harlequin romances and the Christian right. *The Journal of Popular Culture*, 35 (4), 75–87.

Davidson, C. (1985) Reading the romance: women, patriarchy, and popular literature by Radway Janice. Reviewed in *American Literature*, 57 (3), 526–527.

Dixon, J. (1999) *The romance fiction of Mills & Boon 1909–1990s*. London and Philadelphia: UCL Press.

Firestone, S. ([1972] 2001) *The dialectic of sex*. London: Paladin.

Frantz, S. & Selinger, E. (2012) (eds.) *New approaches to popular romance fiction: critical essays*. Jefferson, North Carolina and London: McFarland & Company Inc.

Giddens, A. (1992) *The transformation of intimacy: sexuality, love and eroticism in modern societies*. Cambridge: Polity.

Gilmour, R. & Schwarz, B. (eds.) *End of empire and the English novel since 1945*. Manchester: Manchester University Press.

Gleason, W. & Selinger, E. (eds.) (2016) *Romance fiction and American culture: love as the practice of freedom? Surrey and Burlington:* Ashgate.

Greer, G. (1970) *The female eunuch*. London: MacGibbon and Kee.

Hardens, R. (2012) Borderlands of desire: captivity, romance and the revolutionary power of love. In Frantz, S. & Selinger, E. (eds.) *New approaches to popular romance fiction*. Jefferson, North Carolina and London: McFarland, 133–152.

Hoggart, R. (1958) *The uses of literacy*. Harmondsworth: Penguin.

Hollows, J. (2000) *Feminism, femininity and popular culture*. Manchester and New York: Manchester University Press.

Horkheimer, M. & Adorno, T. ([1944] 1972) *Dialectic of enlightenment: philosophical fragments*. Translated from German by J. Cumming. New York: Seabury.

Huyssen, A. (1986) Mass culture as woman: modernism's other. In Modleski, T. (ed.) *Studies in entertainment: critical approaches to mass culture*. Bloomington and Indianapolis: Indiana University Press, 188–208.

Jackson, S. (1993) Even sociologists fall in love: an exploration in the sociology of emotions. *Sociology*, 27 (2), 201–220.

———. (1995) Women and heterosexual love: complicity, resistance and change. In Pearce, L. & Stacey, J. (eds.) *Romance revisited*. London: Lawrence and Wishart, 49–62.

Jones, R. (1986) Mills & Boon meets feminism. In Radford, J. (ed.) *The progress of romance: the politics of popular fiction*. London and New York: Routledge & Kegan Paul, 195–218.

Light, A. (1984) 'Returning to Manderley': romance fiction, female sexuality and class. *Feminist Review*, 16, 7–25.

Margolies, D. (1982) Mills & Boon: guilt without sex. *Red Letters*, 14, 5–13.

Millett, K. (1970) *Sexual politics*. London: Rupert Hart-Davis Ltd.

Modleski, T. (1982) *Loving with a vengeance: mass-produced fantasies for women*. London: Methuen.

———. (1986) *Studies in entertainment: critical approaches to mass culture*. Bloomington and Indianapolis: Indiana University Press.

Mussell, K. (1984) *Fantasy and reconciliation: contemporary formulas of women's romance fiction*. Westport, CT: Greenwood Press.

Pearce, L. (2007) *Romance writing*. Cambridge and Malden: Polity.

Pearce, L. & Stacey, J. (eds.) (1995) *Romance revisited*. London: Lawrence and Wishart.

Philips, D. (2011) The empire of romance: love in a postcolonial climate. In Gilmour, R. & Schwarz, B. (eds.) *End of empire and the English novel since 1945*. Manchester: Manchester University Press, 114–133.

Radford, J. (ed.) (1986) *The progress of romance: the politics of popular fiction*. London and New York: Routledge & Kegan Paul.

Radway, J. (1983) Women read the romance: the interaction of text and context. *Feminist Studies*, 9 (1), 53–78.

———. ([1984] 1991) *Reading the romance: women, patriarchy, and popular literature*. Chapel Hill and London: The University of North Carolina Press.

Rani, M. (2014) The conflict of love and Islam: the main ingredients in the popular Islamic novels of Malaysia. *South East Asia Research*, 22 (3), 417–433.

Regis, P. (2003) *A Natural history of the romance novel*. Philadelphia: University of Pennsylvania Press.

Rix, R. (2009) Love in the clouds: Barbara Cartland's religious romances. *Journal of Religion and Popular Culture*, 21 (2), p. 2.

Roach, C. (2016) Love as the practice of bondage: popular romance narratives and the conundrum of erotic love. In Gleason, W. & Selinger, E. (eds.) *Romance fiction and American culture: love as the practice of freedom? Surrey and Burlington:* Ashgate.

Ross, M. (2013) "What's love but a second hand emotion?" Man-on-man passion in the contemporary black gay romance novel. *Callaloo*, 36 (3), 669–678.

Snitow, A. ([1979] 2001) Mass market romance: pornography for women is different. In Weisser, S. (ed.) *Woman and romance: a reader*. New York and London: New York University Press, 307–322.

Teo, H. (2014) "We have to learn to love imperially": love in late colonial and federation Australian romance novels. *Journal of Popular Romance Studies*, 4 (2), https://www.jprstudies.org/2014/10/we-have-to-learn-to-love-imperially-love-in-late-colonial-and-federation-australian-romance-novelsby-hsu-ming-teo/.

Weedon, C. ([1987] 1997) *Feminist practice and poststructuralist theory*. New York: Blackwell.

Weisser, S. (2013) *The glass slipper: women and love stories*. New Brunswick, New Jersey, and London: Rutgers University Press.

Wendell, S. & Tan, C. (2009) *Beyond heaving bosoms: the smart bitches' guide to romance novels*. New York: Fireside.

1 What Is Love

> Self-seeking, possessive love (often referred to as 'Eros-love') is the prerequisite for self-giving, submissive love (often called 'agape') and not, as most tradition insists, its necessary opposite. In fact, the more powerful agape-love is, the *more* powerful must be Eros-love, on whose searching energy agape feeds.
>
> (May 2011: 189)

Much has been said and written about love, though to date defining love has not been deemed possible. There has been very little agreement on a uniform definition of love, as it is simply not a concept associated with specific patterns of behaviours or actions (Weisser 2013: 5–6). Various types of love have been distinguished according to the different love objects or recipients, for example, children, spouse/partner, and friends. This book focuses on heterosexual romantic love, the love that two individuals of the opposite sex may share. Love may take various forms based on the location, historical period, and/or culture. It may be an act of gallantry, an abstract idea, or just a desire that each individual is entitled to. For example,

> the psychoanalyst treats it as an individual adjustment to universal infantile desires, the scientist deals with it as a neurochemical phenomenon, the sociologist assumes it is socially adaptive, the philosopher addresses [it] as an abstract concept, the historian focuses on its culturally specific development, and the literary critic analyses the shape and thematics of the narrative itself.
>
> (5)

DOI: 10.4324/9781003432487-2

For Susan Weisser, love is the outcome of a combination of feelings and social constructions and systems. It is

> embedded in the brain as well as the rest of the body, [but also is seen] as a social concept, one with immense personal meaning, as is the body itself. Love is experienced as feeling – or rather multiple feelings, physical, mental, and emotional – labelled within a belief system and positioned within a social system.
>
> (10)

In agreement with Weisser, Stevi Jackson takes a Butlerian approach and suggests that love is a product of social relations and interactions and as such it derives from the process through which individuals are "doing" love (Jackson 2014: 36). According to her, love is subject to one's social milieu, economic resources, class, and position that one occupies in society. Also, she emphasises the fluidity, and therefore the feeling of love, by stating that love is relational as it is structured on the interpretation of one's interaction with others and with culture (36). Similarly, Arlie Hochschild concurs with Weisser and Jackson on the role that culture and society play regarding the feeling of love. She states that the way individuals feel love is dependent on "cultural dictionaries" which consist of what "is pre-acknowledged, pre-named, pre-articulated, culturally available to feel" (Hochschild 2003: 121) or in Jackson's words love is "socially ordered, linguistically mediated and culturally specific" (Jackson 1993: 39). The scholars mentioned here, as well as the feminists discussed below, view love in connection with society and its constructs. Not only are they interested in the way individuals experience this emotion, but also in the power structure within love.

In this book, the term 'romantic love' refers to the Western concept of love and signifies "a specific kind of emotional attachment, that is used as a yardstick to measure something deep, valuable, or enduring against sexual relations that are temporary or casual" (Weisser 2013: 7). This type of love is greatly associated with passion, exclusivity, and monogamy. However, historically marriage and romantic love did not always go hand in hand in the past. In patriarchal societies monogamy was traditionally seen as a way of securing men's access rights to their spouse and their offspring and love was conceived as something which could jeopardise the socially accepted nature of the institution of marriage (i.e. convenience and economic circumstance) (Giddens 1992: 38). As Stephanie Coontz notes, prior to the eighteenth century

> most societies around the world saw marriage as far too vital an economic and political institution to be left entirely to the free choice of the two individuals involved, especially if they were going to base their decision on something as unreasoning and transitory as love.
> (Coontz 2006: 5)

Moreover, Coontz suggests that it was

> only in the seventeenth century [that] a series of political, economic, and cultural changes in Europe [began] to erode the old function of marriage encouraging individuals to choose their mates on the basis of personal affection and allowing couples to challenge outside intrusions upon their lives. And not until the late eighteenth century, and then only in Western Europe and North America, did the notion of free choice and marriage for love triumph as a cultural ideal.
> (Coontz 2006: 7)

Giddens also seems to suggest that there is a connection between marriage and romantic love and the appearance and wider distribution of romantic narratives: "an increasing tide of romantic novels and stories, which has not abated to this day – many written by women – flooded the bookstores from the early nineteenth century onwards" (Giddens 1992: 41). In the nineteenth-century love was perceived as the foundation of marriage and an essential component of a fulfilling relationship between individuals. However, not everyone embraces the idea of romantic love as a way of maintaining a heterosexual relationship. Some feminists (Simone de Beauvoir, Shulamith Firestone, and Andrea Dworkin, amongst others) see romantic love as a delusion and as problematic with regard to patriarchy and a limitation to women's lives. Simone De Beauvoir, for example, views love as the means of a woman's subjugation. Instead of liberating, it enslaves her. Her agency is consumed and absorbed. Rather than being treasured and admired, she becomes a part of him.

> [E]verything she is, everything she has, every second of her life must be devoted to him and thus find their raison d' être; she does not want to possess anything except in him; what would make her unhappy is that he demands nothing of her […] She first sought in love a confirmation of what she was, her past, her personage; but she also commits her future: to justify it she destines it to the one

> who possesses all values; she thus gives up her transcendence: she subordinates it to that of the essential other whose vassal and slave she makes herself. It is to find herself, to save herself that she began by losing herself in him: the fact is that little by little she loses herself; all reality is in the other. Love that was originally defined as a narcissistic apotheosis is accomplished in the bitter joys of a devotion that often leads to self-mutilation.
>
> (de Beauvoir [1949] 2011: 708)

Here, de Beauvoir reflects on the depiction of women in love in the 1940s in France. She evokes a particular idea around conventional romantic love. Her idea of romantic love is similar (but not identical) to the love described in some of the Mills & Boon 'Modern' romance novels examined in this book. The heroine might initially show feminist ideals and a neoliberal identity and does not seek "in love [of the hero] a confirmation of her personage". However, once her emotions develop, she "little by little [*chooses* to lose] herself", a choice which results in her being 'consumed' by the hero. Shulamith Firestone concurs with de Beauvoir. In her words romantic love is "love corrupted by its power context … into a diseased form of love" that maintains male superiority (Firestone [1972] 2001: 139). Moreover, romantic love was considered the locus of gender inequality and women's subordination in marriage (Wollstonecraft [1792] 1975: 118). Similarly, Andrea Dworkin defines love as "a frenzied passion which compels women to submit to a diminishing life in chains" (Dworkin 1976: 105). Over the years, romantic love has been seen as "a kind of false consciousness, against which women should guard themselves" (Smart 2007: 61) and as "an ideological mask for the economic, sexual and physical exploitation of women" (39). Barbara Ehrenreich et al. praise physical pleasure over love and suggest that the latter is used to prevent women from seeking pleasure (Ehrenreich et al. 1986: 195).

However, Christina Nehring takes an opposing position to the above-mentioned feminists and terms romantic love as follows:

> at its strongest and wildest and most authentic, love is a demon. It is a religion, a high-risk adventure, an act of heroism. Love is ecstasy and injury, transcendence and danger, altruism and excess. In many ways, it is a divine madness—and was recognized exactly as that as early as the time of Plato.
>
> (2009: 13)

She argues that it was societal politics that undervalued romantic love:

> Feminism has brought many other good things. It's brought half the human population the right to be ambitious, the right to be political, the right to be sexually playful. One of the few things feminism has not yet brought womankind – and indeed has helped torpedo – is the right to be romantic. All other doors stand open. We can run for president or stay in the nursery; cruise for sex or plan a family. Just about the only thing we cannot do is *love*.
>
> (273)

In this quotation she suggests that feminism, in combination with "materialism, pragmatism and cynicism" (that characterise this post-modern era), transformed romantic love into what she calls "fast love", "non-love" (Nehring 2009: 14), and "a cause for embarrassment" as "[t]o this day, a woman in love is a woman who must relinquish her feminist credentials" (271). Based on this argument, she attempts to reaffirm its lost and misunderstood qualities by proposing "greater trust between genders and fresh daring among lovers" (275).

In the twenty-first century, there appears to be constant media-based pressure on how people should dress, act, behave, and even love. Individuals are bombarded by images of the 'ideal' romantic love in movies, books, songs, and advertisements, and the ideas and perceptions on love that they form are based on westernised romantic love, the type of love that is more often than not described in the pages of a popular romance novel and/or "in Hollywood-like genres" (Nehring 2009: 272). Although it may be accepted that to an extent romance fiction narratives follow a standardised formula, the following sections illustrate that these narratives portray more than one type of love, such as 'confluent' and 'romantic'. The novelty of illustrating a variety of love forms found in romance novels signals the complexity of love and intimate relationships in this post-modern period.

Lust or Love: Confluent vs. Romantic Love

Heterosexual love is a broad term. It could signify romantic, sexual, conjugal, and/or 'confluent' love (Giddens 1992: 62). As the purpose of this section is to examine the love relationship between the two fictional characters of the romance novels, only the romantic (amorous) and confluent (sexual but aromantic) variants of love will be studied further. Romantic love "provides for a long-term life trajectory, oriented to an anticipated yet malleable future; and it creates a 'shared history'" (Giddens 1992: 45). As Giddens notes, romantic love is concomitant with intimacy and a "meeting of souls which is reparative in character" (45). It is reparative as the individuals fulfil each other's lack of self-identity and their coming together therefore signifies a completion of the self as a whole. Romantic love is also closely linked with emotional attachment and transcendence as it idealises the love object and suggests a joint, future development (45). Moreover, it allows individuals to rise above their usual state. Confluent love, as coined by Giddens, is somewhat different from romantic love as it is transient and emphasises the sexual over the emotional. In his words, a 'confluent' or 'pure' relationship is one where

> a social relation is entered into for its own sake, for what can be derived by each person for a sustained association with another; and which is continued only in so far as it is thought by both parties to deliver enough satisfactions for each individual to stay within it.
>
> (58)

It is 'pure' and 'confluent' because the durability of this type of love, and therefore relationship, is dependent on the partners and exists until sexual saturation is reached or the gains of such a relationship no longer satisfy one or the other. Additionally, it is not necessarily based on exclusivity and monogamy.

In the context of the romance genre, novels temporarily provide their readers with desirable, ideal, and imaginary romantic love. This love serves as a form of escapism and sometimes a short-lived emotional fulfilment. According to Radway, unlike in real life, romances honour the emotional aspect. They offer "vicarious emotional nurturance by prompting identification between the reader and a fictional heroine whose identity as a woman is always confirmed by the romantic and sexual attentions of an ideal male" ([1984] 1991: 113). Moreover, by placing the heroine at the hero's centre of attention, these romance stories portray her "as worthy of his concern" and strengthen "her [the heroine and therefore the reader's] sense of self" (113). The majority of these romances end with a happily-ever-after and some sort of betrothal which suggests future development between the protagonists (i.e. a romantic and companionate love relationship).

Bibliography

Coontz, S. (2006) *Marriage, a history: how love conquered marriage*. London: Penguin.

de Beauvoir, S. ([1949] 2011) *The second sex*. H.M. Parshley. London: Jonathan Cape.

Dworkin, A. (1976) *Our blood: prophecies and discourses on sexual politics*. London: Harper and Row.

Ehrenreich, B., Hess, E. & Jacobs, G. (1986) *Re-making love: the feminisation of sex*. New York: Doubleday.

Firestone, S. ([1972] 2001) *The dialectic of sex*. London: Paladin.

Giddens, A. (1992) *The transformation of intimacy: sexuality, love and eroticism in modern societies*. Cambridge: Polity.

Hochschild, A. (2003) *The commercialisation of intimate life*. Berkeley: University of California Press.

Jackson, S. (1993) Even sociologists fall in love: an exploration in the sociology of emotions. *Sociology*, 27 (2), 201–220.

Jackson, S. (2014) Love, social change, and everyday heterosexuality. In Jónasdóttir, A. & Ferguson, A. (Eds.) *Love: a question for feminism in the twenty-first century*. New York and London: Routledge.

May, S. (2011) *Love: a history*. New Haven and London: Yale University Press.

Nehring, C. (2009) *A vindication of love: reclaiming romance for the twenty-first century*. New York: Harper Perennial.

Radway, J. ([1984] 1991) *Reading the romance: women, patriarchy, and popular literature*. Chapel Hill and London: The University of North Carolina Press.

Smart, C. (2007) *Personal life*. Cambridge: Polity.

Weisser, S. (2013) *The glass slipper: women and love stories*. New Brunswick, New Jersey, and London: Rutgers University Press.

Wollstonecraft, M. ([1792] 1975) *A vindication of the rights of woman with strictures on political and moral subjects*. Baltimore: Penguin.

2 The Love Continuum

Taking the definitions of romantic and confluent love discussed in Chapter 1 into account, what can be argued is that in the post-millennial 'Modern' romance novels examined here, *both* love variants emerge and form a continuum[1] that illustrates the progress of love relationships. This continuum is divided into three parts which are termed as follows: pre-personal, semi-personal, and personal. Pre-personal connotes the initial stage of a relationship between protagonists who only share an interest and an attraction for each other based solely on physical appearance. Semi-personal refers to sexual interaction without the disclosure of any feelings. The personal phase of a relationship is when emotions are awakened and acknowledged (i.e. realisation of love).

The sections that follow map this continuum onto the narratives. For this purpose, two romance novels have been selected – *Too Proud to Be Bought* by Sharon Kendrick (2011) and *The Girl He'd Overlooked* by Cathy Williams (2012) – and quotations are provided (from their beginning to happily-ever-after ending) that illustrate every stage of the love continuum. Moreover, to strengthen my argument on confluent love (discussed in the 'Semi-Personal Relationship' section), examples are given from five additional novels. These are: *Surf, Sea and a Sexy Stranger* (Heidi Rice 2010), *Blame It on the Bikini* (Natalie Anderson 2012), *The Notorious Gabriel Diaz* (Cathy Williams 2013), *His Temporary Mistress* (Cathy Williams 2014), and *His Diamond of Convenience* (Maisey Yates 2015).

The novelty of this continuum is grounded in the analysis of the 'Modern' romance novels. Its significance lies in the fact that it contributes to a better understanding of the *different* love types portrayed in the novels. Furthermore, it can be used to evaluate the progress of romantic love in other forms of twenty-first-century popular culture (for example, chicklit narratives and/or rom-coms: *Friends with*

DOI: 10.4324/9781003432487-3

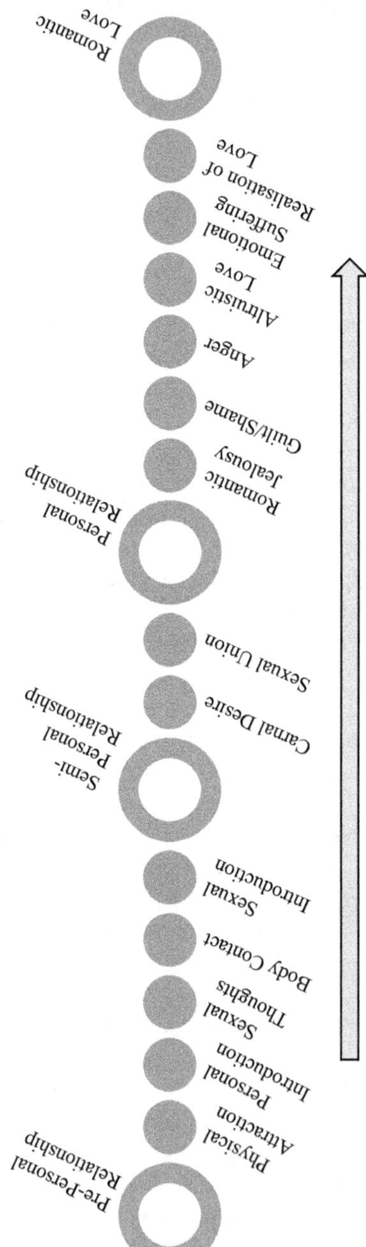

Figure 2.1 Love Continuum
(Source: Author)

Benefits (2011); *The Ugly Truth* (2009); *How to Lose a Guy in Ten Days* (2003)). In the next pages, these three stages of the continuum are discussed in greater detail.

Pre-Personal Relationship

The first stage of this continuum is physical attraction between the protagonists. The heroes and heroines are drawn together based on each other's physical appearance and characteristics. This interest is of an exploratory nature and has a dual function: it is a) personal and b) sexual. It is personal in the sense that the protagonists are intrigued to discover/receive information about their desired object, for example, personal details, occupation, etc. Once the personal is established, the exploratory sexual (i.e. physical) interest follows and arises due to some type of body contact. In romance novels, often the personal is in contradiction with the physical: the personal information received suggests the protagonists should avoid each other, but the physical attraction forces them in the opposite direction (mind/body dualism). It is these touches, accidental or intentional, along with the use of sexual innuendos, compliments, and implicit (unspoken) erotic thoughts that generate and increase the anticipation and excitement of being sexually introduced to each other.

In *The Girl He'd Overlooked* (2012), for example, James Rocci and Jennifer Edwards have known each other since childhood. She had a crush on him for years until on her twenty-first birthday she tried to kiss him but he pushed her away. Four years later she returns to her house to deal with home maintenance issues and finds him there. Regardless of the circumstances under which they meet, and although they have known each other before, their (*re*-)introduction still takes place. That is they see each other through a different lens – both personally and sexually. Their personal (*re*-)introduction is necessary as their living circumstances have changed, their personalities have developed, and their professions (mostly the heroine's) have progressed. After her mother's death, Jennifer spent most of her teenage years close to her father. She didn't "[stray] far from the family home … university just around the corner" (*The Girl He'd Overlooked* 2012: 11). However, now she is an independent, well-travelled, and career-focused young woman: she is "twenty-one years old, with a degree in French firmly behind her and a secondment to the Parisian office of the law firm in which she had spent every summer vacation working" (8). For James professional development was not an easy task either. He

> had taken over his father's company when, in the wake of his father's death six years previously, the vultures had been circling, waiting to snap it up at a knock-down price. At the time he had barely been out of university, but he had skipped the gap year he had planned and returned to take the reins of the company and haul it into the twenty-first century.
>
> (9–10)

Now he is a successful cosmopolitan businessman. Apart from their personal (*re*-)introduction, the sexual (*re*-)introduction is equally important. Their bodies have now fully developed and formed and remind little of their teenage form and shape:

> In the space of four years, she had been seduced by Parisian chic. She had lost weight, or maybe, thanks to her daily run, the weight had just been reassigned. At any rate, the body she had once avoided looking at in the mirror now attracted wolf whistles and stares from strangers and she was not ashamed to wear clothes that accentuated it.
>
> (*The Girl He'd Overlooked* 2012: 27)

In *Too Proud to Be Bought* (Kendrick 2011) the initiation of the hero and heroine's relationship is based on their mutual physical attraction. The introduction takes place at an exclusive, high-class society party which Zara Evans, who is merely a waitress, attends only to showcase her best friend's dress. She is hoping to meet Nikolai Komarov, who is a Russian billionaire, and interest him in her friend's work. Similarly to the novel above, the protagonists' introduction is quite intense:

> [S]he found her eyes drawn unwillingly to a man who was standing at the far end of the ballroom. And suddenly, she couldn't stop looking. It was like seeing a drop of blood on virgin snow – because he stood out from everyone else in the room. His hair was the colour of beaten gold, his eyes were glacially blue and he possessed a hard and arrogant mouth, which spoke of experience and sensuality. In the flesh he was perfect [...] the most intimidating man she had ever seen. His face made her think of a diamond – with its hard, sculpted angles and those cold, glittering eyes [...] Powerful, wealthy tycoon he might be, but, more than anything, he was pure and unbridled masculinity. It felt like

> having all the breath punched from her body as she found herself captured in his cold yet searing gaze.
>
> (*Too Proud to Be Bought* 2011: 10–11)

In this quotation the heroine's interest and attraction for the hero is described as a sudden and irresistible force invading her body ('the breath punched from her body') and mind ('unwillingly', 'couldn't stop looking'). 'Seeing a drop of blood on virgin snow' is an interesting simile that also paints the hero as a man of exceptional beauty, a man who stands out from the rest. Moreover, the description of his hard features ('beaten gold hair', 'glacially blue eyes', 'sensual mouth', 'hard sculpted angles', 'cold, glittering eyes') adds to the idea of his hegemonic masculinity. This detailed description of the hero's appearance also emphasises the significance of the personal (and later physical) introduction as an essential step towards the protagonists' love progression. Nevertheless, just as the heroine's interest is provoked based on the physical appearance of the hero, his does not remain unaffected either. Her presence and her figure attract his attention. It is this uncontrollable physical attraction that brings the hero and heroine closer and offers them a chance to personally introduce themselves.

> He'd noticed her the moment she'd walked into the ballroom in that clinging green gown and he had been watching her ever since. [H]er face wasn't stiffened with Botox and her hair had the natural shine of youth. But it was her body which was the real showstopper. He felt a sudden flare of lust as he acknowledged that her body was absolutely *amazing*. All curves and seductive hollows and none of the gaunt look of the over-dieted. He let his skin gaze drift downwards over her bare shoulders – a skin which gleamed as softly as silk – to where her pert and luscious breasts formed a cleavage which was like an open invitation to a man's lips.
>
> (*Too Proud to Be Bought* 2011: 13)

This passage describes the heroine's appearance which has magnetised the hero's attention. Her portrayal as a natural beauty ('her face wasn't stiffened with Botox', 'natural shine', 'none of the gaunt look of the over-dieted') makes a reference to unrealistic images of idealised beauty and to women who decide on cosmetic interventions to improve their appearance and conform to these ideals. Therefore, the fact that she is natural immediately distinguishes her from other women. Additionally, her body's description is antithetical to the hero's. He is strong, hard, and muscular while she is likened to silk ('softly as silk'). It appears that muscularity equates to masculinity (Arvanitaki 2022) while softness and grace indicate femininity. Also, her appearance (just like his) paves the way towards the personal (and sexual) introduction of the protagonists.

It is this (*re*-)introduction of their (newly developed) selves that ignites the exploratory personal and sexual interest. Even though, primarily, their interest is concealed and expressed only through thoughts, it quickly takes the form of brief body contact.

> What alarmed her were those casual touches, the brush of his gloved fingers against her arm, the feel of his thigh next to hers [...]. Her body had felt alive; her skin had tingled [...] yearning to be touched. It was barely a thought that she had allowed to cross her mind, but she knew it was there. What if, on the spur of the moment, she let her hand linger just a little bit too long on his arm? What if she held his look for too long?
>
> (*The Girl He'd Overlooked* 2012: 53)

In the case of *Too Proud to Be Bought*, the protagonists' sexual interest is expressed through dancing. Sharing a dance at a party allows for evanescent body touches and indicates the beginning of their sexual introduction: the hero's "hands had moved down and were now lying on her hips, the fingers splayed against the silk of her dress with a lazy and proprietary ease so that for a moment it felt as if he were touching the bare flesh underneath" (*Too Proud to Be Bought* 2011: 20). The heroine is also sexually influenced by this short-lived body contact as "she could feel the barely touching sensation of his fingers pressing against her flesh. A shiver of longing rippled over her flesh, a sensation so unexpected and unwanted that she felt the sudden thunder of her heart" (23). Here, her body's reaction to the hero's touch seems to take the heroine by surprise. Moreover, this physical attraction signposts the later stages (semi-personal and personal) of the protagonists' emotional development.

These momentary touches, along with the sexual innuendos and occasional glimpses of nude body parts, complement and give birth to a sexually charged atmosphere. While cutting some trees down to clear them off the power lines, James hurts his back. In pain and immobilised, he is required to ask the heroine to help him get undressed and change into some clean and dry clothes. However, at the sight and touch of his body, the following thoughts are generated in the heroine's mind:

> She didn't have to look at him as she began easing the trousers off. On their downward path, she was aware of black-tight fitting underwear, the length and strength of his legs, his muscled calves. She was in danger of passing out, and even more when she heard his voice in her head telling her that she was a sexy woman.
>
> (*The Girl He'd Overlooked* 2012: 74)

Again, in this quotation the phrase "in danger of passing out" signifies the strong sexual attraction the heroine feels for the hero. The hero is also influenced by her accidental body exposure. When her robe falls open he is offered a view of her nightwear and breasts

> [N]ow he had an eyeful of long, shapely legs and the brevity of a tee shirt that delineated full, firm breasts. Desire for her now slammed into him [...]. James kept his eyes firmly fixed on her face because anywhere else would have been disastrous for the array of responses his body was having in her presence. Those were definitely her nipples outlined against the soft cotton tee shirt. He could see the tips of them. It was just one reason to make sure he looked directly at her face, although even that made him feel a little giddy.
>
> (84)

In *Too Proud to Be Bought* the brief touches in combination with the short previews of the heroine's body also function as accelerators of the hero's sexual interest and an electrified atmosphere "[h]e could see the outline of her legs through the silk of her dress - slender, lean legs – and he felt another sharp ache of desire" (*Too Proud to Be Bought* 2011: 25–26).

Despite the sexual emotions that the protagonists experience, both of them keep their erotic desire and attraction towards the other veiled. However, the authors of these selected novels provide both points of view – the man's attraction to the woman; the woman's attraction to the man – and this creates a more intense sexual atmosphere which in turn makes the romance story more appealing and attracts the readership's interest. The hero and heroine's reluctance in voicing their carnal wishes results in the depiction of physical attraction as unspoken sexual thoughts:

> [h]e couldn't get images out of his mind, images of her in his apartment, images of her looking at him the way he knew he wanted to look at her, images of her turning to him, raising her lips to his, closing her eyes.
>
> (*The Girl He'd Overlooked* 2012: 104)

Also "she leaned against the doorframe and closed her eyes, she could picture James lying on it, wickedly, sensationally sexy, with dark satin sheets lightly covering his bronzed muscular body [...] She blinked guiltily and the image was gone" (87). In addition, the hero's sexual thoughts are also described as follows:

> he *really* wanted her. In fact, he was tempted to start making love to her right now and rid himself of the fever which burned so hotly in his veins. To find some quiet and private corner and where he could thrust deep inside her, while the warm and scented summer surrounded them and she cried her pleasure against his neck. Yet Nikolai knew that timing was everything. And now was not the right time.
>
> (*Too Proud to be Bought* 2011: 47)

In the examples given above, the protagonists go to great lengths to restrain their sexual thoughts. However, their bodies are canvases onto which erotic desire can be painted and consequently, the protagonists' well-kept secrets are quickly revealed. It is following the revelation of their sexual impulse that their semi-personal relationship begins.

Semi-Personal Relationship

The growth of this hidden desire for each other gradually brings down the protagonists' self-imposed barriers. The sexual need and attraction are increasing, leaving the heroes and heroines with no other alternative but to come closer and finally indulge in the (*re-*) introduction of their bodies. In other words, the physical attraction is the driver that takes over and forces them to approach each other. In this case, they enter a semi-personal relationship by sharing their first kiss:

> She closed her eyes on a soft sigh and their mouths touched, a sweetly exploring caress, then he reached both his hands into her hair, brushed his thumbs along her neck and didn't give her the opportunity to surface as the gentle exploration turned into something wonderfully, erotically hungry.
>
> (*The Girl He'd Overlooked* 2012: 108)

In a similar vein, the hero and heroine of *Too Proud to Be Bought* cannot suppress their sexual urges any longer as "now he was kissing her and it seemed the most natural thing in the world to let him. On and on it went, deeper and deeper – like no kiss she'd ever experienced before. It felt like heaven – better than heaven" (*Too Proud to Be Bought* 2011: 82).

With the completion of their first sexual experience (as partners) comes closure but also a new beginning. The state of being simply two individuals with an interest in each other is now gone as they enter a sexual relationship, a 'confluent' love relationship. This 'confluent' relationship is based on carnal desire and sexual gratification (Giddens 1992: 58). In addition, as the quotation suggests there is still a plot impediment that only allows for a temporary sexual relationship:

> He wanted her to quit her job but he had been careful to give her no promises of a future. They would be lovers. He had treated her the same way he had treated all the women he had ever gone out with. Up front announcing his lack of commitment, making sure she didn't get it into her head that long term was part of his vocabulary.
>
> (*The Girl He'd Overlooked* 2012: 127)

The plot impediment in this case is not only the hero's lack of commitment but also his inability to see her as different from the other women. Similarly, in *Too Proud to Be Bought* there is also a hindrance to overcome and that is the hero's inaccessibility:

> I don't do love. I don't want to marry – and I certainly don't want children of my own. And neither […] do I want some woman on a mission – however sweet and sexy she might be – thinking that she's going to change my mind for me.
>
> (*Too Proud to be Bought* 2011: 132)

He makes it explicitly clear to her that no feelings will be involved in this relationship:

> I can offer you a great deal, Zara – and if you want to continue with the arrangement we have, then nothing would please me more. You make a great – if somewhat unconventional – mistress. But I'll never marry you – and I'll never give you a baby.
>
> (133)

Victoria Calder and Dmitri Markin from *His Diamond of Convenience* also share a confluent relationship. Both of them are aware that emotions should not be involved in this equation: "what she wanted had nothing to do with romance or love. [...] It had everything to do with desire" (*His Diamond of Convenience* 2015: 104). The hero also sees this situation from the same perspective "[t]here was nothing he could offer Victoria beyond tonight, or perhaps beyond a physical relationship that would extend only until their business dealings were done" (120). Therefore, they agree to maintain their relationship purely on a physical level:

> I cannot give you any more than this.
> I understand.
> When our arrangement is over, this will be over, too. You can be my lover in New York, and through the event in London. But once the ownership of your father's boutiques is returned to your family, this will end.
>
> (143)

The concept of a confluent relationship is also evident in *The Notorious Gabriel Diaz*. The hero has made his intentions clear from the start. Their relationship should be strictly limited to sexual gratification: "I'm not the kind of guy who's into commitment. I treat my women well ... better than well ... but I never encourage them to think that there's any more than what I'm prepared to give" (2013: 71). The romance novel *Surf, Sea and a Sexy Stranger* depicts the confluent relationship of Ryan King and Maddy Westmore. To avoid any complications, the hero

> was usually so clear with women about what he wanted out of a relationship. And what he didn't. He set boundaries and he never crossed them. No point in confusing things and setting yourself up for an ugly scene further down the line.
>
> (2010: 96)

With this in mind, he suggests a relationship which would satisfy his and the heroine's bodily desires:

> What do you say to a no-strings affair? We spend a few weeks exploiting the great sexual chemistry between us and then go our separate ways. And nobody gets hurt.
> […] No strings. No promises. Just great sex?
> That's correct […].
> All right, […] I think that would be fun.
>
> (97)

All the novels examined here have a period of sexuality without commitment as the protagonists embark on a casual (confluent) relationship without expecting anything in return. Although these statements [mostly made by the heroes] may sound harsh and do not fulfil the heroines' emotional needs and/or hopes, they indicate the heroes' honesty. In this part of the novels, the heroes are represented as unwilling to commit, and emotionally invest themselves in a relationship with the heroines, as love has little or no significance for them.

However, this confluent love relationship is not always welcomed by both protagonists as the emotional awakening for the heroines starts almost immediately after the sexual activity. "He told her repeatedly that he couldn't get enough of her and, with every smile, and every touch, she fell deeper and deeper into love" (*The Girl He'd Overlooked* 2012: 117). For the heroes, sexual intercourse generates lust; for the heroines, it creates love. Romance novels here show a gender asymmetry in experiencing (and perceiving) love and make the same point as Byron: "man's love is of man's life a thing apart/ 'Tis woman's whole existence" (*Don Juan*, Canto I). What can be derived here is that the romance novels examined in this book are still very standardised and very traditional in their representation of women as dominated by love. They are aware of the consequences of revealing their feelings and often withhold themselves from expressing their wish for any future development with the heroes. Sacrifices have to be made, and the suppression of their emotions leads to the heroes' existence in their lives. A confluent love is not always a self-made choice, and faced with the possibility of losing the heroes, the heroines pretend to be in agreement. "James liked her. He certainly adored her body. That was where the story ended. He had warned her off looking for anything more than sex and she had *successfully convinced him* that they were both on the same wavelength" (128) (emphasis added) and "we both know that this is just a physical attraction. It'll pass in time and we'll both move on so why involve other people when there's no need? [...] Let's just have fun. And no complications" (133). The heroine, in *Too Proud to Be Bought*, is aware of the hero's reluctance to let his emotions develop. He "never offered her anything more than the physical attraction between them which burned so fiercely. Not even when they'd got back together after their break. The brief episodes of closeness they'd shared hadn't really deepened" (*Too Proud to Be Bought* 2011: 170). Scared that she might lose him, she agrees to continue with this façade. However, she knows

> that she ha[s] neither the strength nor the inclination to end it. What had started out as fierce physical attraction between them had grown into something she'd neither wanted nor expected. [...] And somewhere along the way, she realised, she'd fallen in love with him.
>
> (*Too Proud to Be Bought* 2011: 133)

As in the novels mentioned above, in *His Temporary Mistress* (2014) what keeps Damien and Violet together is the physical attraction. Both are aware of the raison d'être of their 'arrangement' which is no more than lust and sexual satisfaction. To avoid any misunderstanding (in this case, the awakening of feelings) the hero makes his intentions clear: "You know how the ground lies. I'm not looking for any kind of commitment. Been there, done that, won't be revisiting that particular holiday hotspot in the foreseeable future. But what's going on right now … mind-blowing" (2014: 132). Initially the heroine in this novel shares the hero's view and sees their relationship purely based on physical attraction and herself as "a grown woman who was more than capable of handling a sexual relationship with a man to whom she was inexplicably but powerfully attracted" (139). However, with the acknowledgement of her developing feelings for him comes the possible termination of their relationship. It is the fear of losing the hero that makes her "maintain the façade of being as casual about what they had" (142).

What is exciting here for the experienced romance reader is that the revelation of the heroines' feelings about the hero might jeopardise their casual relationship and, consequently, the novels' standardised formula of ending with a betrothal or an optimistic ending. Another example that exemplifies the different perceptions of love between the genders is the following: while "every compliment he paid her had to do with sex, with her body, with the physical", emotions of "love had been quietly settling like cement and now she felt constricted, unable to move and as fragile as a piece of spun glass" (150). Once again where the hero experiences carnal desire and lust, the heroine sees love. In the same manner, the romance novel entitled *Blame It on the Bikini* (Anderson 2012) presents the protagonists' involvement in a confluent relationship (which is later transformed into a romantic one). What is surprising here is that it is the heroine who is the initiator of the sexual relationship. This implies an evident exchange of gender roles with regard to love, sex, and commitment as it is usually the hero who is unwilling to commit. Also, in the following examples, the romance novel is making a nod to feminism as it shows a heroine who no longer has to be virginal and can be open about sex: "I don't want a relationship, and I don't want a fling. But I've changed my mind about the one-night thing" (2012: 125), "I don't want anything more. I'd never expect promises from you. I understand this. […] And you know I can't give more either. This isn't going to be anything more for either of us" (126). Therefore, with an agreement to keep emotionality out of the equation, both Brad and Mya enter into a confluent relationship:

> So what do you suggest – no rules?
> No rules. […]
> You're offering to be my love slave? You'll do whatever I want?
> You take pleasure from me and I'll take pleasure from you.
> (150)

Unlike in the previous novels, here it is the hero who is getting emotionally attached to the heroine. His 'no strings attached' behaviour – "[h]e'd positioned himself as her bed-buddy – painted himself into a corner as her 'good-time guy'. And was that so bad? A few minutes of fun here and there in an otherwise hardworking life? He was the king of quick'n'fun, wasn't he?" (157) – has started to change as now

> he cared for her more than he'd like and the reality was he didn't stand a chance. There was no room in her life for him. […] He'd

played the playboy role too well for too long for her to see him any other way. He supposed it served him right

(157)

and "He didn't want to hear what *little* she wanted from him. He'd made the bed. But now the bed wasn't enough for him" (163). What can be observed from this section is that in the twenty-first-century 'Modern' romance novels examined here, a temporary confluent relationship occurs between the protagonists. This sexual attraction is the necessary stepping stone to the emergence of feelings and the realisation of love. Although the male character (due to his emotional inaccessibility) is commonly represented as the one who seeks a carnal relationship, in the case of *Blame It on the Bikini* there is a reversal of gender behaviours. Here, the novel promotes the heroine as the initiator of a physical rather than emotional relationship. Nevertheless, regardless of who is the instigator of this type of love, both women and men develop feelings as a result of sexuality. The culmination of the semi-personal (sexual) relationship can trigger a personal (emotional) relationship and is the next stage on the continuum.

Personal Relationship and the Process of Emotional Development

After the sexual union of the protagonists, romance novels allow for a number of variant feelings to be explored. The first is jealousy, succeeded by guilt, which, although it is usually linked to an event that occurred in the past, is closely related to the relationship between the hero and heroine. Next, anger makes its appearance and finally altruism as a form of love. The combination of these feelings constitutes a gradual emotional development of the hero and heroine towards the realisation of (feelings of romantic) love. Prior to examining each of these emotions separately, a difference in the protagonists' emotional development should be noted. The heroine's emotional growth is different *in pace* to the hero's. Soon after their sexual encounter she begins to develop feelings for the hero. He, on the other hand, as an emotionally inaccessible man, only realises that he loves her just a couple of chapters before the end of the romance fiction. This leads to the conclusion that, in the post-millennial 'Modern' romance novels examined here, the depiction of women and men with regard to love differs. While men are often depicted as cynical and concerned only with their own interests and sexual gratification, women are characterised as individuals with more emotional attributes (than the heroes) who associate sexual activity with feelings. Regardless of the speed of the emotional development, both fictional characters experience similar emotions.

Romantic Jealousy

Jealousy between two partners, or romantic jealousy, is a combination of cognitive, behavioural, and affective emotions that surface when the relationship is threatened by the (possible) existence of a third party (Guerrero et al. 2005: 243). This mixture of emotions consists of anger, sadness, guilt, and passion, amongst others (234). In other words, romantic jealousy is defined as

> a complex of thoughts, emotions, and actions that follows loss of or threat to self-esteem and/or the existence of quality of the romantic relationship. The perceived loss or threat is generated by the perception of a real or potential romantic attraction between one's partner and a (perhaps imaginary) rival.
>
> (White and Mullen 1989: 9)

Many consider the outcome of expressing jealousy to be negative. However, Guerrero and Andersen (1998) propose that this feeling could result in a "positive effect" on the relationship. For example, in her work *Romantic Jealousy: Causes, Symptoms, Cures*, psychologist Ayala Pines suggests that romantic jealousy stops individuals from taking their partners for granted as it is the trigger and facilitator of an individual for showing more excitement and commitment to a relationship (1998: 80).

In the romance fiction narratives examined in this book, jealousy seems to function as an indication of emotional growth between the protagonists. For the hero, jealousy is closely related to masculine self-esteem. Regardless of whether the third party in the relationship belongs in the past or present, the hero is intrigued to find out more: "on the spur of the moment, he looked up Patric Alexander on an Internet search engine, hardly expecting to find anything because artists were a dime a dozen and few of them would ever make it to the hall of fame" (*The Girl He'd Overlooked* 2012: 42–43). The reason behind this masculine curiosity lies in the fact that achievement and success form the basis of the masculine identity (Gilligan 1982: 163). Pines and Friedman suggest that men "are more likely to respond with jealousy when their masculine self-esteem is threatened" (Pines and Friedman 1998: 67). Therefore, the hero is jealous and disappointed when he discovers that the heroine's ex-boyfriend is praised by the media as

> the new up-and-coming talent in the art world. Patric was already garnering a loyal following and a clientele base that ensured future success. The picture was small, but [the hero] zoomed into it and found a handsome fair-haired man surrounded by a bevy of beautiful women.
>
> (43)

With the realisation that Patric was more than what he was expecting, and despite the fact that his relationship with the heroine is at an early stage, the hero feels threatened and competitive towards him and tries to discover possible negative personality traits in an attempt to devalue him. "He certainly looked on top of the world in those pictures I saw of him. Big grin, lots of hot babes around him" (85).

With the thought of a romantic rival in mind, individuals may also express their jealousy through feelings of sadness and insecurity (Parrott 1991: 13–14). As the novel progresses, and after the establishment of their sexual (confluent) love, the heroine is determined to end things with him. His words signal sadness, "You've found someone else. Is that it?" (141) and his thoughts indicate self-doubt, "How long had she been contemplating *that*? Had there been some other man lurking in the background? One of those fictitious sensitive, emotionally savvy guys she had once told him made ideal partner material?" (141).

For the hero in *Too Proud to Be Bought*, jealousy carries signs of ownership as "he hated seeing her going off each day to wait on men who were doubtless eyeing the luscious swell of her breasts instead of what was on the tray she was offering them" (*Too Proud to Be Bought* 2011: 124). The hero's jealous feelings indicate a gendered idea about masculinity and possession which places the heroine in a subordinate position; that of the owned. In this case, the hero's actions (in the expression of a love relationship) resonate with Goldman's words and her representation of masculinity in the seventies

> [t]he male [...] insists on playing the part of a conqueror, since he has been told that women want to be conquered, that they love to be seduced. Feeling himself the only cock in the barnyard, or the bull who must clash horns in order to win the cow, he feels mortally wounded in his conceit and arrogance the moment a rival appears on the scene – the scene, even among so-called refined men, continues to be woman's sex love, which must belong to only one master.
>
> (Goldman 1972: 172)

Thus, it is this type of jealousy – which derives from the need to possess the heroine – that awakens the hero's emotions.

In *The Girl He'd Overlooked*, the heroine is also jealous and bears feelings of rivalry towards James's ex-girlfriends. She imagines his secretary as "someone young, pretty and adoring, following him with her eyes and working overtime just to remain in his company, and suddenly [is] sick with jealousy" (2012: 90–91). Later, when he discusses the possibility of offering a certain work task to someone, Jennifer's imagination is once more occupied, "throwing up images of a little blonde thing, cute and brainy, simpering and doing whatever she [is] asked of her" (94). Similarly to the hero, she also tries to belittle his past choices of partners "those are the sort of girls you've always been interested in. Blonde, big hair, small, very high heels and very tight dresses" (39–40). Jealousy quickly turns into an act of comparison and an indicator of her self-doubt and self-esteem. In bed with him, she voices her insecurity regarding her body as she states "I'm not one of your Polly Pockets" (108). In the chosen 'Modern' romance novels discussed here, the heroines' jealousy is represented differently from the heroes'. The latter's jealousy derives from the need to *possess* and *own* the heroines. The former's jealousy is the result of their self-projection. In *The Girl He'd Overlooked*, the heroine compares her body with the body figures of his ex-partners. Knowing that she does not conform to the stereotypical beauty ideal (for example a thin, toned body, slim waist, etc.) she mentally puts herself through a comparison process which exalts their slim figures over her curvy shape.

Zara is also envious towards Nikolai's ex-girlfriends because of a picture of him with a French actress in the newspaper. The picture was "taken near some stunning looking house, with a woman beside him *who was even more stunning*" (*Too Proud to Be Bought* 2011: 168) (emphasis added). Jealous of the actress's beauty, she loses control of her emotions and bursts out "How was Marie-Claire? […] The French actress you're so close to" (*Too Proud to Be Bought* 2011: 173). Her reaction also portrays elements of hurt as she compares herself to the actress's beauty. Additionally, she has already started to invest emotionally in their relationship. It is her emotional engagement to him as well as her failure to conform to the ideal beauty standards that makes her accuse him of unfaithfulness without any evidence and betrays her true feelings.

Regardless of the jealousy-related feelings (i.e. sadness, insecurity) that emerge with (and because of) it, jealousy also shows evidence of emotional growth and development. Moreover, it provides the readership with an emerging sense of caring and sharing between the hero and the heroine. It is the first sign of progress, taking the relationship from a confluent stage, and with this an ambivalent future – which is mostly based on sex and the fulfilment of carnal desire – towards a more romantic variation of love.

Guilt and Shame

Guilt is the next step in the 'personal relationship' phase of the love continuum and plays an equally important (to jealousy) role in the emotional development process of the hero and heroine of romance novels. Guilt is important because it brings the hero and heroine closer. Guerrero et al. note that "the action tendency associated with guilt is to try and correct, repair, or otherwise make amends for one's behaviour" (Guerrero et al. 2005: 247). As this section will demonstrate, it is through their attempts to rectify their mistakes that the protagonists get to know each other and share experiences. Due to the similar connotations they carry, guilt is often confused with shame. However, there are certain distinctive differences. To ensure the clarity and validity of my argument – that guilt is part of the emotional development process – guilt and shame will be explained and differentiated prior to the textual analysis of the romance narratives.

Guilt and shame are self-conscious emotions. Self-conscious emotions are closely linked to one's sense of self and understanding of societal relationships. They act as self-regulators and provide "internal feedback about a specific goal, expectation, or standard that has been violated" (Beer and Keltner 2004: 127). Tangney et al. conceptualise shame as "an affective reaction that follows public exposure (and disapproval) of some impropriety or shortcoming" (1996: 1256) while guilt is seen as "an adaptive moral affect that stems from people's negative evaluation of their own behavior (or lack of behavior) when an internalized standard has been violated" (Bruno et al. 2009: 490). In greater detail, the differences between the two notions are the following: shame is a social emotion (deals with the socially objectionable and intolerable) and "is caused by external sanctions emanating from other people or institutions" (Wallbott and Scherer 1995: 474). Guilt, on the other hand, is an emotion that stems from within. Also, in contrast to guilt, shame is an emotion linked to the entire self, a "global self-evaluated" emotion (Lutwak et al. 2003: 909), which is related to a specific action or type of behaviour (Lewis 1971). In addition, shame is "ultimately about punishment" (Gilbert 2003: 1225). Overall, Teroni and Deonna summarise the differences between guilt and shame by arguing that "[g]uilt is a personal emotion, regulating one's behavior through one's own standards. By contrast, shame is social since it regulates one's conduct through other people's standards" (2008: 729). In other words, shame is associated with the evaluation of the self, whereas guilt is tied up with the self-criticism for a specific event, action or behaviour.

In the context of twenty-first-century 'Modern' romance novels, there are numerous cases in which the heroes and (mostly in a traditional Greek context) the heroines experience shame because of socially disapproving actions in the past (e.g. in *The Cozakis's Bride* the heroine is a child conceived out of wedlock) or due to public exposure (e.g. in *A Girl Less Ordinary* where the heroine feels shame as the press gets hold of her relationship with the hero; she is also ashamed of her past self). However, with regard to the *emotional development of the protagonists,* what the hero and heroine experience is guilt, rather than shame. Their sense of guilt derives from certain actions or behaviours of the past for which now they feel remorse. Frequently guilt arises from alienation from home and parents, falling out with someone from the familial and/or social environment, incidents with ex-partners, etc. For example, Jennifer feels guilty about her behaviour towards the hero. What causes that feeling is her mishandling of the situation she has found herself in: "While she had been reluctantly catering to his demands, and not bothering to hide the fact that she wasn't overjoyed at having him under her roof, he had been suffering in silence" (*The Girl He'd overlooked* 2012: 73). Her guilt originates from the fact that she should have helped and taken care of him while so far she has only shown him that he is an unwelcomed distraction and a burden. Looking after someone should not be a chore but rather an act of kindness and humanity. Furthermore, she also feels guilty because during his stay at her home "she had been a miserable friend, taking out her insecurities on him when he had done nothing but try and fix the gaping hole four years of absence had left in their friendship" (83). Zara Evans also feels guilty due to her unfair judgement of the hero. Her anger was triggered by a picture of the hero with an actress at a party while they were on a break. Due to her lack of trust in him, she

> had accused him of infidelity – she had wanted to believe the very worst of him – was it any wonder that their relationship hadn't deepened when she had been sitting on the sidelines just waiting for him to step out of line? Yet he had never given her any reason to believe that he was interested in other women, had he?
>
> (*Too Proud to Be* Bought 2011: 176)

Despite the heroes' attempt to regain lost ground, the heroines experience remorse and embarrassment, which derive from their uncaring and insensible behaviour towards the heroes.

In the novels examined here, and contrary to the heroines' feeling of guilt due to present actions, the source of the heroes' remorse is usually rooted in their past. James's relationship with a woman from his workplace has deeply affected him as he found out that she used him to get a promotion. Since that shocking discovery, he has lost his trust in women and avoids any kind of commitment. James feels guilty for two reasons: firstly, for not spending more time with his mother, especially after his father's death. He admits that "[he] should have been at home. At least, [he] should have been at home more than [he] was. Instead, [he] was being seduced by Anita Hayward of the long red hair and slandering green eyes" (*The Girl He'd Overlooked* 2012: 124). Rather than supporting his mother, he was dedicating most of his time to his partner. Secondly, he feels guilty because, if it were not for his ignorance and naïveté, he would not have been hurt and therefore he would not have made "a rational decision to steer clear of anything called uncontrolled emotional development" (125). Nikolai has also had bad experiences in the past. His abandonment by his mother, as well as her shameful acts (selling her body for money) when he was just a small boy, has had a negative impact on his relationships.

He does not get emotionally involved with any woman as he believes that wealth and love cannot coexist in a relationship: "After her [his mother's] desertion – the precious bond between mother and son forgotten in her pursuit of wealth – he had discovered a whole world of ambitious and deceitful women out there" (*Too Proud to Be Bought* 2011: 39). However, when he finds out that his mother never stopped trying to find him and did not leave with a rich man as he believed, he feels guilty. He is also regretful for assuming that the heroine was a money-hungry woman who was involved with him because of his wealth. Because of these past events, the heroes are not able to trust the heroines, to allow themselves to develop emotionally, and to create a relationship based on love.

In all of the above cases, the protagonists' guilt functions as an evaluation and self-criticism of their actions based on their internal convictions. The main difference between the heroes and the heroines of the novels examined here is that the heroines' sense of wrongdoing is linked to the heroes whereas for the heroes guilt is triggered by incidents of the past. And although the heroes might have made mistakes in the past, it is the heroines who now face the consequences of these choices.

In general, like jealousy, guilt should not necessarily be seen as a negative emotion. Many researchers suggest that guilt functions as motivation for individuals to acknowledge their wrongdoings and attempt to correct them (Keltner and Buswell 1996: 156; Lewis 1971: 30; Tangney et al. 1996: 1257). Guilt also leads to emotional self-disclosure: that is the engagement of the individual in "reparative actions" such as apologising or even discussing/sharing their guilt with someone else (Tangney et al. 1996: 1257). With reference to the romance novel, the heroes exhibit a growing insight into their self, undergo a (self-) disclosure and (self-) evaluation process when they unveil their sense of guilt, and share their experiences with the heroines. By doing so, they are relieved as they find comfort in the heroines. Moreover, guilt – and particularly the emotional disclosure that comes with it – constitutes a hint of familiarity and closeness between the protagonists. Along with these past experiences, the heroes share a newly founded intimacy with the heroines. At first glance, guilt may seem like an obstacle between the hero and the heroine, though it is its redeeming and restorative nature that brings the protagonists closer to a mutual emotional development.

Anger

Anger often emerges in occurrences of jealousy (Sharpsteen 1991: 38). It is considered to be associated with aggressive behaviour (verbally and/or physically), especially in romantic relationships (Sugarman and Hotaling 1991: 101). The feeling of anger emerges from the thwarting of one's aims or plans by someone or something (Anastasi et al. 1948: 246, 247). In *The Girl He'd Overlooked*, the hero shows signs of verbally aggressive behaviour when the heroine announces that she is pregnant with his child. Shocked by the unexpected pregnancy he angrily says: "You can't be. You're using contraception. I've seen that little packet of pills in the bathroom. Are you telling me that you've been pretending to take them?" and adds "We used a condom. We were protected. We were always protected. This is madness. I can't believe I'm hearing any of this" (142). His anger is a result of the realisation of the inevitable change that will occur to his life, plans, status, and independence. He will no longer be carefree and independent. He will be a father and he will be forced to "throw his neatly ordered life out of sync for ever" (144). With reference to jealousy, anger occurs when the goal and/or continuity of a romantic relationship between the two protagonists is threatened (Shaver et al. 1987: 1077) What 'threatens' their shared future, and therefore triggers his aggressiveness, is not the pregnancy *per se* but the heroine who wants to leave him solely *because* of her pregnancy. Angry with the heroine's decision he asks in disbelief "You're going to have my baby and you greet me with the opening words that you want out of this relationship?" (*The Girl He'd Overlooked* 2012: 144) His anger grows when she explains that she will not enter in a marriage for the wrong reasons (i.e. the baby):

> I can't marry you because you think it makes sense. When I get married, I want it to be for all the right reasons. I don't want to settle for a reluctant husband who would rather be with someone else but finds himself stuck with me.
>
> (146)

For her, marriage is a matter of the heart. The heroine's answer infuriates him: "How healthy would it be for our child to grow up without both parents there? Because that's something you need to consider! This isn't about you and your romantic notions of fairytale endings!" (146)

As Guerrero et al. note "jealous individuals who experience anger more intensely than fear may be more likely to attack than escape" from a difficult situation (Guerrero et al. 2005: 235):

> Let me provide you with an alternative scenario. Our child grows up in a split family and in due course finds out that both of us could have been there but you wouldn't have it because you were determined to look for Mr Right, who may or may not come along. And if he does coming *[sic]* along…well, I'm telling you right now that he won't be involved in bringing up my child because *I'll fight for custody.*
>
> (147) (emphasis added)

This is precisely what the hero resorts to. Unable to prove a point and persuade the heroine that this marriage could be for the child's benefit, he verbally attacks her. Nikolai's anger is provoked by Zara's wish for their relationship to deepen. She believes that relationships are not static but "are supposed to grow […] – not stay packed in ice" (*Too Proud to Be Bought* 2011: 146). However, she is aware that a possible development of their relationship is against his loveless life so she decides to leave him as she "can't be involved with someone who doesn't allow himself to feel anything!" (142) Her emotional demands irritate him as his plans are thwarted (i.e. a relationship free of any emotional commitment). Anger is evident in his reaction:

> so is this leading to some kind of ultimatum you've been cooking up? You threaten to leave me and hope that the diamond ring and promise of commitment comes swinging your way? As a strategy, I have to tell you that it's been used before – but it never works.
>
> (142–143)

He expresses his disappointment in Zara by stating

> I've given you more than I've given any woman and I don't know whether there's anything left to give – because I get nothing back. Nothing! You affect not to care about my money or power and yet, deep down, I think that you despise them. They're all you see – instead of the man underneath – the man who stupidly thought you might be able to look beneath all the trappings.
>
> (175)

Despite her inability to see his true self beneath the wealth, he does not walk away. On the contrary he verbally attacks her: "If I get such an empty reception at home, then maybe I'll try to find a little comfort elsewhere. And let's face it. [...] if I'm going to be accused of something I might as well get the benefits of it!" (175–176).

Overall, on these occasions, the heroines act as the catalyst of the heroes' anger. If the heroines had remained passive and had not expressed their true desires and longings, the heroes would not have expressed their anger and verbally attacked or threatened them, and therefore their feelings would have remained disguised. However, if that were the case, these romance stories would not follow the archetypal standardised structure of romance fiction: "boy meets girl. Holy crap, shit happens! Eventually, the boy gets the girl back. They live Happily Ever After" (Wendell and Tan 2009: 11). The purpose of anger in these novels is equally important to the feelings discussed above, in that (in the romance context) anger is an expression of deeply concealed wishes, goals, and plans. It is the clash of contrasting opinions that contributes to the emergence of what Regis calls the "point of ritual death" (2003: 30–38) or, in the words of Wendell and Tan, the "Big Misunderstanding" (2009: 100). Both of these terms refer to the specific moment of the protagonists' relationship where "an external conflict [...] causes internal conflict" (101). At this point in the novel, the reader starts "to doubt the intelligence of the couple and, what's worse, their ability to sustain a happy ending of their own" (101). However, anger should not only be examined from a negative perspective. On the contrary, anger – even if expressed by voicing clashing beliefs and opinions –– can also signal a process of exploring each other's personality and can *still* lead towards the development of a romantic relationship between the hero and heroine. Furthermore, anger constitutes the second part (or twist) in the plot development – misunderstanding, *falling out*, and reunion of the protagonists – and indirectly suggests the beginning of its resolution.

Altruistic Love

Altruism and masochism are two terms that are often falsely equated (Rousseau 1991: 20). According to Paula Caplan, women are thought to be masochist in nature as they postpone their self-gratification in the process of putting others' needs first (Caplan 1993: 40). Masochism is generally conceptualised as the act of taking pleasure in one's own pain or humiliation. It has been mostly related to women and is seen by some as an innate characteristic and a key concept for understanding women (Bernstein 1983: 467–468) and has been characterised as their "anatomical destiny" (Deutsch 1930: 51). A rather extreme and sexist perspective is that of Freud who supports that masochism "is truly feminine" (Freud 1933: 116). On the other hand, others note that both men and women, due to a number of biological, psychological, and cultural factors, can show signs of masochism (Simons 1987: 591). Masochism does not only refer to physical but also emotional (psychic) pain (Tosone 1998: 416). Altruism (or self-sacrifice), on the other hand, "is seen as giving-up on one's own well-being for the sake of others" (Rousseau 1991: 20). Moreover, Mary Rousseau differentiates between altruistic love and masochism by suggesting that the former "does not require any diminution or destruction of one's self" and adds that "one who would love another altruistically, wishing his good to him for his sake, puts himself at the service of that good" (20).

In the context of romance fiction, the developing love between the protagonists is of an altruistic nature as it exhibits the self-sacrifice of one's needs and the prioritising of the other's [needs] without considering the consequences of such an action. Nevertheless, because of the sacrifice of one's self and wishes, protagonists at times may endure (emotional) pain. Therefore, romantic (or altruistic) love, and the self-sacrifice that exists in it, is "suffering, not joy, as evidence of true love" (Sanchez 2011: 3). For example, in the case of *The Girl He'd Overlooked,* the heroine shows signs of altruistic love when she asks for the termination of the relationship shortly after she discovers she is pregnant with his child. On the one hand, she is struggling with herself and the feelings she has for him (i.e. she is emotionally hurt). On the other, she respects his wish of not committing to any long-lasting, meaningful relationship (i.e. sacrifices herself). Thus, the heroine is an individual who, by forgoing her wishes, delays her gratification of entering into a marital union with him and sharing a future. Instead, she chooses to satisfy his needs and not let him change his status as "he was a man accustomed to freedom of movement and independence, fundamentally unanswerable to anyone" (171). In other words, she relinquishes her needs for his benefit: "You didn't ask for this to arise and I'm not going to punish you [...] by putting you in a position of having to stand by me whether you like it or not" (144).

However, her emotional martyrdom does not end there. She is left emotionally hurt as her initial feelings of interest and sexual attraction have grown into something bigger. What she actually wants is a shared future. The heroine is left to suffer in silence: "how could she explain that a baby needed more than a couple united by passion? Or even, for that matter, friendship?" (144–145) and "How could she hold herself at a distance from him? How could she deny that what they had together was good? Beyond good?" (167). What the above quotation suggests is that love in these twenty-first-century 'Modern' romance narratives is not so much about passion. It is not about friendship either. Passionate (sexual) and amicable love are welcomed by both fictional characters. Yet, what they really desire is the combination of the two: a companionate and reciprocal love. Therefore, her choice not to express her wishes and her self-sacrifice – although it might have not collided with passion and friendship – is what victimises and deprives her of experiencing romantic love.

The hero in his novel is also described as a self-sacrificing man. Despite his fear of commitment he wants to be fully involved with her pregnancy and his unborn child. He is not subconsciously putting himself in a difficult, uncomfortable, and troublesome position, rather he is fully aware of the sacrifices he has to make and although he "wanted to run as fast as his feet could take him to the farthest corner of the earth because fatherhood, for the man who couldn't commit, would have been the albatross around his neck" (156), he does not. On the contrary, since she has declined his marriage proposal, he suggests the compromise of sharing a house for the child's sake. Given that this is a man who refrained from any emotional involvement due to his past experience, cohabiting with the heroine is a major step but he is "ma[king] sure to conceal any trepidation from her" (172). His altruism becomes more evident when "with a sense of duty no longer in the equation, living together had struck him as more of a commitment" (171). However, he temporarily puts his needs aside while trying to fulfil hers. She needs security and a stable environment and he is ready to give up his independence to help her. The altruism exemplified here both by the hero and heroine signifies a sense of looking after and caring for each other even if this contradicts their own wishes.

Zara is a self-sacrificing woman who experiences (a form of) self-oppression by putting aside her needs for the possibility of future development with the hero. She has paused her life to fulfil his desires:

> she'd boxed herself into a corner the moment she had agreed to start living with Nikolai. Her future was as uncertain as it had ever

> been – maybe even more. There was no possibility of going away to agricultural college to restart her course – because then she would see hardly anything of him. And he wouldn't put up with that, she recognised. He just about tolerated her waitressing work- as long as it didn't eat into their evenings together.
>
> (*Too Proud to Be* Bought 2011: 165–166)

Aware that she can only exist in association with the hero, she accepts the role of his mistress however degrading this may be "[l]ove had weakened her and desire had sapped what strength was left, allowing her to morph into being a wealthy man's commodity; his mistress" (*Too Proud to Be Bought* 2011: 163). Again, here the heroine's altruism and love for the hero are depicted through putting her wishes aside and making certain decisions about her life that accommodate his needs (e.g. not attending her college in order to spend more time with him). By doing so, the heroine willingly puts herself in a subordinate position in their relationship.

Thus, in the twenty-first-century romance fiction narratives examined in this book both the heroes and heroines experience (emotional) pain when they consciously put themselves in this predicament. To reach this state, they postpone their self-gratification and attempt to fulfil each other's needs. In this case, self-sacrifice is not solely a depiction of emotional suffering. It is a strong and intense well-hidden sense of caring and dependence (since both of them exist in association with each other). However, it should be noted that in the examples cited above the self-sacrifice experienced by the hero and heroine is not of the same degree. The compromises that the heroines are called to make (for example, being a single parent and/or not receiving further education) seem greater than the heroes' compromises (in this case, moving in and/or starting a relationship with the heroines due to fear of commitment). Regardless of the extent to which one postpones his/her wishes, dreams, aspirations, and needs, self-abnegation is the means through which the altruistic nature of love replaces its egotistic side. With the emergence of self-denial comes the realisation of love, which is explored in the next section.

Realisation of Love

The realisation of love in most romances usually takes place after the occurrence of a significant – and often unfortunate – event. This event, which takes various forms, precipitates the appreciation and recognition of the feelings and actions of the protagonists and therefore contributes to the realisation of love. A noticeable finding is that these heroines are more attuned to their feelings as they realise their love for the heroes after their first few sexual encounters while the heroes often reach this stage just before the end of the novel. To overcome their emotional remoteness, an unfortunate event is required. In the case of *The Girl He'd Overlooked,* the cause of acknowledging his feelings towards her is the possibility of miscarriage. It is shortly after the overcoming of this plot impediment that the heroines realise the heroes' true feelings for them. For example, in *The Girl He'd Overlooked*

> He had been affectionate, supportive, reassuring and, as she had always known, wonderfully funny and entertaining. He had returned from work early so that she could put her feet up while he had cooked. He had put up with Ellie coming round every few days and had only given her the occasional dry look when her best friend had launched into colourful stories about her love life. He had indulged her sudden taste for soaps on television and brought her cups of tea whenever she wanted.
>
> (177)

Similarly, the effect of this unforeseen event makes the heroes accept and come to terms with their feelings. For example, in *Too Proud to Be Bought*, Nikolai realises his feelings for Zara after she declares her love for him in front of a major social gathering. Accustomed not to show any emotions, he remains silent while she runs away. When he finds her, he offers an explanation regarding his inability to reciprocate any feelings: "my reaction was something which was bone-deep – the lessons I learned in childhood don't suddenly disappear – even if you want them to. Early on, I discovered pretty quickly that it was necessary to block out high emotion" and goes on to declare his love

> After you'd gone, people began to cluster around me – with looks of sympathy on their faces, as if something terrible had just happened. And that's when I realised that something terrible would happen, if I didn't find you and admit what's been building in my

> heart and in my mind for so long. Only I had to come close to losing it before I could find the courage to express it.
>
> (*Too Proud to Be Bought* 2011: 182)

Regardless of the outcome of the event, they express their desire of a shared future: "I want to marry you, Jennifer" (*The Girl He'd Overlooked* 2012: 178), "I know I made it clear from the start that I wasn't into long-term relationships and I had the history to prove it. My life was my work and I couldn't foresee a time when any woman would take precedence over that" (180). Other quotations also indicate the protagonists' desire for a shared future: "if you would do me the honour of becoming my wife?" (*Too Proud to Be Bought* 2011: 183), "I was lost and lonely as a little boy and I never really learnt how to love because nobody had ever shown me how. And no one did … until I met you" (183).

Shortly after the realisation of his love, he discovers that his actions have been dictated by his feelings and wonders how the realisation had not taken place earlier. In this moment of recognition of, and insight into, his feelings, he admits that he "should have known from the very second [he] started thinking about [her] and houses in the same breath that [he] had fallen in love with [her]" (*The Girl He'd Overlooked* 2012: 182).

Whereas for the heroes this may come as a surprise, that is not the case for the experienced romance readership. Accustomed to reading popular romance fiction and due to their trained eye, the readers are able to identify little things such as gestures, thoughts, and actions as indicators of a possible happy ending. On the contrary, heroes (mostly) and heroines (to a lesser degree) need a sudden, upsetting, and unfortunate event to realise their dependence on, and feelings for, each other. Nonetheless, the heroines' doubts and insecurities do not cease to exist only because his feelings have been revealed. It is precisely this moment when the necessity for saying "I love you" – followed by words that indicate a future: "a whole lifetime wouldn't be enough to tell you just how much" (*Too Proud to Be Bought* 2011:183) and "I'm asking you to be the lifelong love of my life" (*The Girl He'd Overlooked* 2012: 183) – comes into place as it works towards eliminating any last reservations the heroines might have regarding the heroes. Knowing that the heroines, through their own altruistic love, have emotionally 'tamed' the heroes (Krentz 1992: 113), they focus on their future development as a couple.

Note

1 Unlike Regis (2003) who analyses romance novels based on the main elements that constitute the story (society defined, the meeting, the barrier, the attraction, the declaration, the point of ritual death, the recognition, the betrothal), the novelty of this continuum lies in the analysis (and unfolding) of the romance novels based on the emotions that the protagonists experience.

Bibliography

Anastasi, A., Cohen, N. & Spatz, D. (1948) A study of fear and anger in college students through the controlled diary method. *Journal of Genetic Psychology*, 73 (2), 243–249.

Andersen, P. A. & Guerrero, L. K. (eds.) (1998) *The handbook of communication and emotion: research, theory, applications, and contexts.* San Diego: Academic Press, 155–188.

Anderson, N. (2012) *Blame it on the bikini*. Richmond, Surrey: Harlequin Mills & Boon.

Arvanitaki, E. (2022) *Masculinities in post-millennial popular romance*. New York and London: Routledge.

Ashton, L. (2012) *A girl less ordinary*. Richmond, Surrey: Harlequin Mills & Boon.

Beer, J. S. & Keltner, D. (2004) What is unique about self-conscious emotions? *Psychological Inquiry*, 15 (2), 126–170.

Bernstein, J. (1983) Masochistic pathology and feminine development. *Journal of the American Psychoanalytic Association*, 31, 467–486.

Bruno, S., Lutwalk, N. & Agin, M. A. (2009) Conceptualizations of guilt and the corresponding relationships to emotional ambivalence, self-disclosure, loneliness and alienation. *Journal of Personality and Individual Differences*, 47, 487–491.

Caplan, P. (1993) *The myth of women's masochism*. Toronto: University of Toronto Press.

Deutsch, H. (1930) Significance of masochism in the mental life of women. *International Journal of Psychoanalysis*, 11, 48–60.

Freud, S. (1933) Femininity. In Strachey, J. (ed.) *The standard edition of the complete psychological works of Sigmund Freud.* Vol. 22. London: Hogarth Press.

Giddens, A. (1992) *The transformation of intimacy: sexuality, love and eroticism in modern societies.* Cambridge: Polity.

Gilbert, P. (2003) Evolution, social roles, and the differences in shame and guilt. *Social Research*, 70 (4), 1205–1230.

Gilligan, C. (1982) *In a different voice*. Cambridge: Harvard University Press.

Goldman, E. (1972) Jealousy: causes and a possible cure. In Shulman, A. K. (ed.) *Red Emma speaks: selected writings and speeches by Emma Goldman.* New York: Random House.

Graham, L. (2000) *The Cozakis bride*. Richmond, Surrey: Harlequin Mills & Boon.

Guerrero, L. K. & Andersen, P. A. (1998) The experience and expression of romantic jealous. In Andersen, P. A. & Guerrero, L. K. (eds.) *The handbook of communication and emotion: research, theory, applications, and contexts.* San Diego: Academic Press, 155–188.

Guerrero, L. K., Trost, M. R. & Yoshimura, S. M. (2005) Romantic jealousy: emotions and communicative responses. *Personal Relationships*, 12 (2), 233–252.

Keltner, D. & Buswell, B. N. (1996) Evidence for the distinctness of embarrassment, shame, and guilt: A study of recalled antecedents and facial expressions of emotion. *Cognition and Emotion*, 10, 155–171.

Kendrick, S. (2011) *Too proud to be bought.* Richmond, Surrey: Harlequin Mills & Boon.

Krentz, J. A. (ed.) (1992) *Dangerous men and adventurous women.* Philadelphia: University of Pennsylvania Press.

Lewis, H. B. (1971) *Shame and guilt in neurosis.* New York: International Universities Press.

Lutwak, N., Panish, J. & Ferrari, J. (2003) Shame and guilt: characterological vs. behavioral self-blame and their relationship to fear of intimacy. *Personality and Individual Differences*, 35, 909–916.

Parrott, W. G. (1991) The emotional experiences of envy and jealousy. In Salovey, P. (ed.) *The psychology of jealousy and envy.* New York: Guilford, 3–30.

Pines, A. (1998) *Romantic jealousy: causes, symptoms, cures.* New York and Oxon: Routledge.

Pines, A. & Friedman, A. (1998) Gender differences in romantic jealousy. *The Journal of Social Psychology*, 138 (1), 54–71.

Rice, H. (2010) *Surf, sea and a sexy stranger.* Richmond, Surrey: Harlequin Mills & Boon.

Rousseau, M. (1991) *Community: the tie that binds.* Maryland and London: University Press of America.

Sanchez, M. (2011) *Erotic subjects: the sexuality of politics in early modern English literature.* New York: Oxford University Press.

Sharpsteen, D. J. (1991) The organization of jealousy knowledge: romantic jealousy as a blended emotion. In Salovey, P. (ed.) *The psychology of jealousy and envy.* New York: Guilford, 31–51.

Shaver, P. R., Schwartz, J., Kirson, D. & O'Connor, C. (1987) Emotion knowledge: further explorations of a prototype approach. *Journal of Personality and Social Psychology*, 52 (6), 1061–1086.

Simons, R. (1987) Psychoanalytic contributions to psychiatric nosology: forms of masochistic behavior. *Journal of the American Psychoanalytic Association*, 35 (3), 583–608.

Sugarman, D. & Hotaling, G. (1991) Dating violence: a review of contextual and risk factors. In Levy, B. (ed.) *Dating violence: young women in danger.* Seattle: The Seal Press, 106–118.

Tangney, J. P., Miller, R. S., Flicker, L. & Barlow, D. H. (1996) Are shame, guilt, and embarrassment distinct emotions? *Journal of Personality and Social Psychology*, 70 (6), 1256–1269.

Teroni, F. and Deonna, J. A. (2008) Differentiating shame from guilt. *Consciousness and Cognition*, 17, 725–740.

Tosone, C. (1998) Revisiting the "myth" of feminine masochism. *Clinical Social Work Journal*, 26 (4), 413–426.

Wallbott, H. G. & Scherer, K. R. (1995) Cultural determinants in experiencing shame and guilt. In Tangney J. P., Fischer, & Kurt, W. (eds.) *Self-conscious emotions.* New York: The Guilford Press.

Wendell, S. & Tan, C. (2009) *Beyond heaving bosoms: the smart bitches' guide to romance novels*. New York: Fireside.

Williams, C. (2012) *The girl he'd overlooked.* Richmond, Surrey: Harlequin Mills & Boon.

——— (2013) *The notorious Gabriel Diaz*. Richmond, Surrey: Harlequin Mills & Boon.

——— (2014) *His temporary mistress*. Richmond, Surrey: Harlequin Mills & Boon.

Yates, M. (2015) *His diamond of convenience*. Richmond, Surrey: Harlequin Mills & Boon.

Conclusion

From Confluent to Romantic Love

As noted in the introduction, love has long been the epicentre of scholarly discussions. Some, such as Firestone, have described it as a delusion and a destructive force while others, such as Nehring, view it as a liberating act which could be mutually enjoyed and bring transcendence for both sexes. In this book, the emotional development of the hero and heroine has been discussed through the construction of a love continuum. This three-phase continuum marks an original contribution to the comprehension of the steps that the fictional characters take towards the realisation of love. Additionally, it indicates the transformation from confluent to romantic love. The first stage of the relationship between the two protagonists is the physical attraction and a personal and physical interest which leads to the entering of a confluent love. Confluent love is a relationship between two heterosexuals based on the sexual rather than the emotional aspect. The emergence/awakening of emotions signifies the termination of confluent love. These emotions *do not necessarily appear in this order or have the same degree of intensity* and function as different phases on the same love progress continuum: romantic jealousy, guilt, anger, self-sacrifice, realisation of (romantic/companionate) love. Romantic jealousy indicates an emerging sense of caring which is replaced by guilt. Guilt brings closeness, intimacy, and sharing, which result in reducing one's emotional distress and/or pain. Anger is subsequent to guilt and offers a way of voicing wishes, aims, goals, and plans that protagonists may have for each other. Anger also denotes a clash of opinions in the process of getting to know each other better. Finally, through the postponement of one's self-gratification for someone else's needs, an altruistic type of love surfaces that of romantic (and companionate) love. In de Beauvoir's words, romantic love

DOI: 10.4324/9781003432487-4

> [m]ust be founded on reciprocal recognition of two freedoms; each lover would then experience himself as himself and as the other; neither would abdicate his transcendence, they would not mutilate themselves; together they would both reveal values and ends in the world. For each of them, love would be the revelation of self through the gift of self and the enrichment of the universe.
>
> ([1949] 2011: 723)

In concluding, *confluent love* could be seen as synonymous with Eros because of its egotistic and selfish nature. As Pearce notes, "(sexual) desire to possess the beloved necessarily outweighs any concern for his or her well-being" (2007: 7). Eros connotes the initial feeling, the passion, love at first sight. It lasts as long as the object of one's desire remains unfamiliar. Conversely, *romantic love* symbolises Agape. Based on mutual understanding, sharing, commitment, trust, and respect (hooks 2000: 7–8) Agape is something substantial, and for one to experience it, self-centredness, selfishness, and narcissism have to be utterly removed from the emotional equation. Ultimately, where Eros requires distance, intensity, passion, and jealousy, Agape embraces a sense of caring, protecting, familiarity, and warmth. Therefore, one can suggest that the post-millennial 'Modern' romance novels examined here maintain and place emphasis on the (traditional and Western) notion of romantic love as the fulfilment of one's self. However, they also embrace modernity and introduce the idea of confluent love – an aromantic relationship based on lust – by indicating that sex constitutes an equally essential step towards the realisation of emotions and the actualisation of a romantic relationship between two individuals.

Bibliography

de Beauvoir, S. ([1949] 2011) *The second sex*. H.M. Parshley. London: Jonathan Cape.

hooks, B. (2000) *All about love: New visions*. New York: William Morrow and Company.

Pearce, L. (2007) *Romance writing*. Cambridge and Malden: Polity.

Index

For Product Safety Concerns and Information please contact our EU representative GPSR@taylorandfrancis.com
Taylor & Francis Verlag GmbH, Kaufingerstraße 24, 80331 München, Germany

www.ingramcontent.com/pod-product-compliance
Lightning Source LLC
LaVergne TN
LVHW010942110826
845149LV00013B/2714

* 9 7 8 1 0 3 2 5 5 8 3 1 8 *